Osprey Modelling • 8

Modelling Panzer Crewmen of the Heer

Mark J Bannerman

Consultant editor Robert Oehler • *Series editors* Marcus Cowper and Nikolai Bogdanovic

First published in Great Britain in 2006 by Osprey Publishing
Midland House, West Way, Botley, Oxford OX2 0PH, UK
443 Park Avenue South, New York, NY 10016, USA
Email: info@ospreypublishing.com

ISBN-10: 1 84603 132 X
ISBN-13: 978 1 84603 132 8

Page layout by Servis Filmsetting, Manchester, UK
Typeset in Monotype Gill Sans and ITC Stone Serif
Index by Glyn Sutcliffe
Originated by United Graphics Pte Ltd, Singapore
Printed and bound in China by Bookbuilders

06 07 08 09 10   10 9 8 7 6 5 4 3 2 1

A CIP catalogue record for this book is available from the British Library.

FOR A CATALOGUE OF ALL BOOKS PUBLISHED BY OSPREY MILITARY
AND AVIATION PLEASE CONTACT:

NORTH AMERICA
Osprey Direct, c/o Random House Distribution Center, 400 Hahn Road,
Westminster, MD 21157, USA
E-mail: info@ospreydirect.com

ALL OTHER REGIONS
Osprey Direct UK, P.O. Box 140, Wellingborough, Northants, NN8 2FA, UK
E-mail: info@ospreydirect.co.uk

www.ospreypublishing.com

Photographic credits

The photographs that appear in this work were taken by Mark
Bannerman unless otherwise indicated.

Acknowledgements

My thanks go to: Prof. Brian Wildfong, Claude Moreau, Taesung
Harmms (Alpine Miniatures), Denis 'Pyro' Allaire, Garfield Ingram,
Arthur 'Love Me Like a Reptile' Sekula, Daniel 'Bond' Munoz, Paul
'Who the heck is Jennie?' Bacon, Chris Roy (R.I.P.), Dave 'ME 109'
Browne, Ron Volstad, Nikolai at Ilios Publishing, Ulf 'Gold for
Sweden!' Anderson, John Rosengrant and Jim Sullivan (S&T
Products), MIG Productions, Alasdaire Johnson (EU Small Shop),
Roger Saunders (Hornet & Wolf), Woody at Archer Fine
Transfers, the kind folks at Royal Models, M.A. Mori, Neil Stewart,
Steen Johansen, 'more-grumpy-than-ever' John and 'no-so-chatty-
anymore' Mike at Maritime Hobbies and Crafts, Dave and Sherry
Brown at Hornet Hobbies, Dave 'Comic Relief' Bailey, the MMM
Crew – and last but certainly not least Mum'n'Dad, my bro' Paul
'Hey There Big Boy!', and my very patient and merciful wife
Elizabeth.

Contents

Introduction

A wonderfully detailed and beautifully finished armour model can easily be let down if accompanied by a poorly painted figure. All too often, armour modellers spend enormous energy and time bringing their AFVs to life with realistic weathering, expensive accessories and a scenic base, then spend very little time painting the figures that go with it. In many cases, figures become an afterthought. This is a shame, because while not every viewer will know exactly what your model is supposed to look like in real life, everyone knows what a human being is supposed to be. Inevitably, some viewers' opinion of the accuracy of the armour model will depend on the overall realistic appearance of the figure.

The addition of scale figures helps provide depth, weight and realism to a model. A well-painted figure can even distract the viewer from a mediocre model. But to this end, painting and working with figures continues to be most armour modellers' worst nightmare, even though building and painting scale armour is far more demanding and time-consuming.

The purpose of this manual is to provide tips and techniques for building, converting and painting World War II German army Panzer crew figures. To add variety, several award-winning modellers will share their own techniques and style. The main themes include how to paint different uniforms using enamels and oils, converting and scratch-building figures, as well as painting heads.

Success in figure painting can only be reached by applying, attempting and comparing one technique to another, thus determining which methods work best for you, and from this, developing your own personal style. For this reason, there are no hard-and-fast rules for painting figures. However, the key to success lies in the 'three Ps': practice, patience and perseverance.

While I have always considered myself first and foremost an armour modeller, my intention has always been to attain a level in my figure painting that allows me to safely add figures to my models without taking away from the kit being presented. This continues to be my philosophy, and for this reason, this manual is really an armour modeller's guide to painting figures, and has been written from this perspective. The approaches in this manual are, by and large, the same techniques used on armour models, with some small variations and slight modifications.

Most of the tools required for figure modelling are the same as those used for armour modelling.

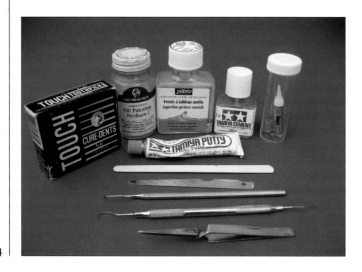

The many types of Panzer uniform offer a wide choice of schemes that are, with small modifications, equally applicable to other uniform types, such as the Panzer uniforms of the Luftwaffe, Waffen-SS and the Polizei. The techniques presented in this manual are also generic enough to allow you to apply them to any other figure size, subject or period. There has been much documented and published on the uniforms and insignia of the German Panzer and assault gun crews of the Third Reich. However, this manual is about building and painting figures, and only a brief explanation of the uniforms being depicted will be described.

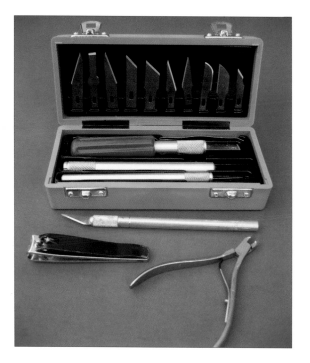

Good quality cutting tools are necessary. The nail clippers are ideal for clean removal of small parts from plastic sprues and resin carrier blocks.

The most important tool required for painting figures is an assortment of various-sized brushes ranging from a small size 5/0 to a larger size 2 or 3.

The tools of the figure modeller

The tools and materials required for modelling figures are the same as those for modelling tanks (scalpels, putty, glues, sandpaper, files and tweezers). However, there are a few additional requirements that need to be discussed.

The most important tool required for painting figures – regardless of the paint being used – is an assortment of various-sized brushes. There are hundreds of brushes available on the market with prices ranging from very cheap to the obscenely expensive. Brushes are made with natural bristle, natural hair or synthetic fibres. Bristle hair and natural hair are similar, but have two major differences: natural hair has a single individual point, while bristle has a number of natural tips, which makes the bristle less flexible but more durable.

Many will argue that expensive and long-lasting brushes are the only option for successful figure painting. While I agree that quality sable brushes are excellent tools, I tend to believe that less expensive brushes will serve equally well. The key to finding a very good brush is less about finding the brush with the smallest tuft of hairs, and more about finding a brush that has a nicely tapered point.

Brush sizes start at 5/0 or smaller, and run to 1 and 2 and beyond, with the higher numbers being larger brushes. The price is almost always contingent on the point of the brush. Most of the brushes I purchase at my local art store are good quality, and for the price of one expensive sable brush I am able to purchase five or six brushes that will probably last two to three years. If one of my 'no-name brand' brushes dries accidentally full of paint, my replacement cost is minimal.

As an added note, oils and enamels are not typically harsh on brushes, and with proper care, any brush should last a very long time. Proper care of your brushes requires a few easy steps: keep paint from getting in or on the metal that holds the bristles, clean your brush thoroughly with the proper brush cleaner for the type of paint you are using, never clean brushes used for metallic paints in the cleaner used for other colours, and always store brushes in a container with bristles up.

With the exception of the round brushes, the brush tips all have a nice taper and finely pointed tips. The key to keeping brushes from flaring is to properly clean the brush and then lightly bring the tip of the brush to a fine point using saliva applied with your finger.

Before the painting process begins, it is important to apply a coat or two of primer to a figure – regardless of whether the figure is white metal, plastic or resin. A conversion piece may be made up of a variety of materials, each with its own natural colour. A coat of primer will even out the surface and give a good working base on which to apply other colours. A primer of a light colour will also greatly help in identifying glitches, sink holes and seam lines. Priming also avoids different materials used on the model reacting differently to subsequent paint. Most fillers and putties will absorb the first coat of paint, which seals them, thereby preventing them from absorbing further coats. Lastly, primers provide a surface for paint to adhere to. The most common and popular primers are the aerosol type offered by Tamiya and Citadel Warhammer. A large canister of primer should allow for priming up to 10 to 15 figures, and is well worth the cost.

I mostly use oils for painting flesh on figures. Oil paints are vivid, and slow drying, which allows ample time to make corrections. Oil paints are not hazardous to breathe, and tend not to emit strong odours. Different brands of oil paint can easily be intermixed without any negative chemical reactions, and the average drying time of most oil paints is anywhere between two and seven days. I do not have a preferred brand, as all of the oil paints on the market are quality paints. Some of the better-known oil paint brands include Rembrandt, Winsor & Newton Artist's Oils, Van Gogh and Daler-Rowney Georgian oils. All four of these brands are readily available at most art stores, and each has a wide range of colours with high pigmentation and excellent clarity of colour. Winsor & Newton also offers a lower grade line (Winton), which offers a smaller range of colours and are less expensive.

While I sometimes use enamel paints for painting flesh, I use these exclusively for painting World War II uniforms. Enamel paints are fairly tough and resistant to handling, and are usually colourfast (they do not change colour with time). Enamels are solvent-based and the vapours can be a little nasty if used in large quantities. My preferred choice of enamels is Humbrol. Humbrol provides the largest selection of colours (more than 100 colours in the matt range), is carried by most hobby stores and is relatively inexpensive. This paint dries to a matt finish, has a slower drying time than acrylics and can easily be mixed with oil paints to create a larger variety of tones and colour values.

An equally important piece of equipment is some form of optical magnification. Working with figures requires focusing the eyes on a very small area, and the exacting nature of the hobby will typically necessitate some visual aid. Various companies offer magnification devices, such as the Optivisor. This contraption has true optical glass lenses that resist scratching and can be worn over regular prescription glasses. I have found that the best standard magnification is a '5' (the 5 stands for 5 Dioptre magnification). Other powers (2, 3, 4, 5, 7, 10) are either too weak (2, 3 and 4), or too strong (7, 10) – resulting in headaches over long painting sessions. Of course, much depends on the individual.

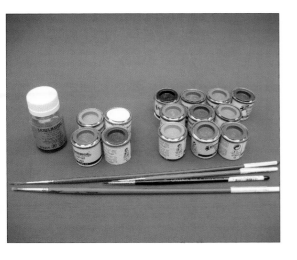

These are the Humbrol enamel paints I use for figure painting. The four tins on the left side are the colours I use for mixing flesh tones (Natural Wood 110, White 34, Wine 73 and Flesh 61). The matt colours on the right side are those I use for uniforms. I also use Model Master and Testors thinners for thinning enamel paints.

I use oil paints for mixing flesh tones. Different brand oil paints can easily be inter-mixed without any negative chemical reaction. My preferred mix includes Winton Burnt Umber, Rembrandt Gold Ochre, Van Gogh Titanium White and Winsor & Newton Burnt Sienna.

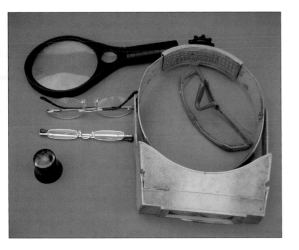

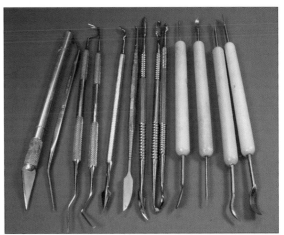

Some form of magnification aid will help considerably, such as the Optivisor with 5 Dioptre, inexpensive reading glasses with 1.25 magnification, strong reading glasses with 1.75 magnification, a Jeweller's loupe with 5X magnification, a hand-held magnifier and the all-important protective eye-glasses when filing resin or metal or when using a Dremel tool for drilling and sanding.

A somewhat daunting-looking collection of tools that can be used for sculpting figures. It is not necessary to have all of these tools and one only needs a good scalpel and one scriber to do the work.

As an endnote, most of the images in this book were taken with a Canon PS45 digital camera with magnification filters. The close-up images of the painting process were shot using four or six 100-watt lightbulbs. I discovered using several hundred watts of intense lighting was not the most flattering means to illustrate the process, but it provides you with a close-and-clear perspective through the painting process. Once the projects in this manual were finished, the figures were then photographed under regular room lights to provide you with a better appreciation of how the finished figures would typically appear under normal conditions.

A selection of resin figures by (left to right) Yoshi, Wolf, Mori, Wolf and TANK. Note the convenient carrier block attachment points on resin figures – under the boots. A small jeweller's saw is very handy for removing these large blocks.

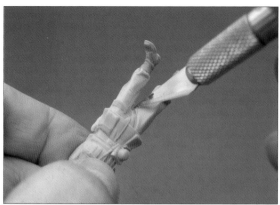

The 90-degree scraping action of a sharp scalpel blade will remove seams and surface blemishes.

White metal figures are heavy and depending on how you opt to position the figure in its final resting spot, it is beneficial to drill a hole up into one of the heels and place a small metal post or large pin to allow the figure to stand on its own weight.

Resin heads in various stages of completion. I usually have a dozen or so heads on the go at any one time. The bottom row comprises heads that have been primed and/or base-coated and the upper row features heads that are nearing completion.

Getting started

With thousands of figures on the market, it is worth discussing, in very general terms, the various types of figure available, how to select a suitable figure and how to prepare a figure for painting.

Figure types

The most popular, inexpensive and readily available figures are made of injection moulded plastic. The typical set contains four to eight figures, usually broken down with separate upper torso, arms, heads, helmets and legs. Plastic figures offer ease of assembly, many conversion possibilities and an overall consistency of scale among manufacturers. The disadvantage is that plastic figures are not quite as crisp in detail as their more expensive white metal and resin cousins. However, many of the new releases by Tamiya, Tristar and DML are exceptional in crispness of detail, and these continue to be the best value for money.

The second most popular choice among modellers is resin figures. Resin figures are generally superior in detail, and are considerably easier to work with when removing surface blemishes, casting seams or flash. The disadvantages are potentially hazardous dust from sanding seams and removing attachment plugs, and the wide variation of scale among different manufacturers. On this last point, a 1/35-scale figure from one company may be quite a bit bigger or smaller than that of another, which can make mixing figures from different resin manufacturers cumbersome. Despite scale irregularities, I will freely mix and match different-sized figures because, in real life, there are shorter and tall people. However, I always use standard-size equipment, helmets, accessories and weapons from one of DML's excellent accessory and weapon sets. Using same-sized accessories on different-sized figures will go a long way to bringing the scale of each figure closer. Some of the more popular companies offering good quality resin figures are Wolf, Artisan Mori, S&T, Alpine Miniatures, Royal, Verlinden, Ultracast and Warriors.

White-metal figures are a bit of a rare find in the 1/35-scale armoured realm, but they do exist. They are generally very well sculpted and cast, and offer some of the best figures on the market. The disadvantage of white metal is that they are not as easily converted, and the weight of a figure will almost always require a pin drilled up through the heel of a boot to allow the figure to stand on its own weight. Companies offering white-metal figures include Hornet and Takahashi.

Choosing a figure

Selecting a figure is about personal choice. Some look for uniform accuracy, others look for clarity and sharpness of surface detail or the level of sculpting of the head. Whatever your criteria, examine the figure carefully. An off-centre eye socket or flattened nose will not look any better once it is painted. Try to look beyond the superbly painted figure on the box art and determine if the figure has the detail, pose and overall appeal you are seeking. Search for a review of the figure on the internet. I typically ask other modellers for their opinion at club meetings or via discussion groups. The golden rule to finding a good figure is that the most expensive figures are not necessarily the best.

Preparing a figure for painting

Regardless of the material composition, a figure will always require a good scrubbing with liquid soap and water to remove casting agents. Most modellers

ABOVE LEFT AND RIGHT
A trooper of Panzer Regiment 6.
(Courtesy Neil Stewart Collection)

skip this all-important step. Removing the casting oils will help prevent mishaps such as flaking paint or glossy blemishes.

I have yet to find a figure that did not require some sanding or filing. For all figures, the light scraping motion of a hobby knife along a surface will remove seams and surface blemishes. Seams that fall inside folds or in hard-to-reach areas can be removed with a small piece of folded fine-grit sandpaper. Different-shaped metal files work well for removing seams on resin and metal figures, but are less practical on plastic figures because the rubbing motion tends to quickly gunk up the files.

With the figure cleaned up, dry-fitting parts to ensure a neat fit is a critical step before actually applying glue on the joints. Small bits of Blu-Tack or putty are an excellent means of testing the overall fit before applying glue. For attaching parts to a plastic figure, liquid glue works very well (such as Testors or Tamiya), and has the advantage of allowing the modeller to fiddle a bit before the glue 'melts and sets' the two joints. For resin figures, you should either use cyanoacrylate (superglue) or epoxy glue. For white metal, I strongly recommend you use epoxy glue. In all instances, apply the glue sparingly and only to one of the joints being glued, not both. Keep the head and belt accessories unattached until after the main body of the figure has been painted.

With the figure glued, some of the joints may need putty or a similar product to fill voids or small gaps. I use a fast-drying car filler, but equally effective products are Tamiya or Squadron putties. Another interesting medium is small bits of plastic sprue that have been immersed in liquid glue. The glue will melt the plastic. With a brush, the 'liquefied' plastic can be brushed into the area and can literally be shaped in place.

THIS PAGE AND FOLLOWING PAGE More period photos of Panzertruppen from Panzer Regiment 6. They are wearing the black wool uniform. (Courtesy Steen B. Johansen Collection)

Painting black uniforms: shadows and highlights

Subject:	*Panzertruppen (armor troops), Poland, 1939*
Modeller:	*Mark Bannerman*
Skill level:	*Intermediate*
Base kit:	*Takahashi white metal figure (TK 06)*
Scale:	*1/35*
Additional detailing sets used:	*Hornet Head*
	Warriors arms
	Archer Fine Transfers
Paints:	*Citadel White primer*
	Humbrol Enamel: Black
	Humbrol Enamel: Flesh
	Humbrol Enamel: White
	Humbrol Enamel: Brown Bess

The earliest uniform worn by Panzer crews was manufactured in black wool and issued in 1934. It consisted of a double-breasted, short-waisted jacket and full-length trousers with tapered legs. The jacket collars were large, with pointed tips, and the top three buttons were generally left undone so that the tunic could be opened at the top. The army and Waffen-SS tank crews wore similar style jackets, but the army tank crew jacket's front was cut at a slant, the lapels were larger with pointed ends, and a centre seam ran up the middle of the back of the jacket.

The army tank crew field jacket also had piped collars in the branch of arms colour, with pink being the most common (for the armoured branch – other colours were golden yellow for Panzer reconnaissance, lemon yellow for Panzer signals, and alternating black and white for Panzer Pioniere). A white-metal *Totenkopf* ('death's head') badge was pinned in the centre of each collar tab, which was also piped in the same colour as the collar. The national eagle emblem (*Hoheitsabzeichen*) was sewn to the right breast. There were different pattern jackets, with the visual changes being in the size and shape of the collars and the addition of buttonholes.

Aside from the dark grey tricot shirt and black tie, the most recognizable feature of the early-war Panzer uniform was the floppy black Panzer beret (*Schutzmutze*). This beret consisted of a helmet covered in an oversized black cloth, with a large insignia wreath and national emblem woven on the front of the beret. This beret was phased out in early 1941, although wartime photos show it being worn after this date. For this feature, I wanted to depict a Panzer crewman in the Polish campaign.

Black provides the added challenge of applying subtle and realistic contrasts between shadows and highlights. Fortunately, the degree of shading required for painting black is greatly reduced compared to lighter colours and the results are far more forgiving and easier to attain. Black uniforms also represent the largest percentage of tank crew uniforms worn in most branches of the Panzertruppen of World War II, making this an excellent subject in this first introductory feature.

I opted to use a white-metal 1/35-scale offering by Takahashi. Before beginning work on the figure, I drilled a 10mm-deep hole into the figure's boot heel, leaving

The basis of my project is a Takahashi white-metal figure in 1/35 scale.

ABOVE The spares box resin arms were temporarily applied to the torso using Blu-Tack. It is always worth doing two or three dry runs to ensure a good fit of parts.

ABOVE RIGHT Car (auto) filler was used to fill any area where small gaps are evident. In this case, car filler was placed inside the small gap between the joint of the arms and shoulders. Liquid glue was applied over the joints to smooth out the filler. I also sanded down the moulded-on collar tabs.

RIGHT The figure received two light applications of Tamiya white primer. Allow the first coat to dry thoroughly before applying a second coat and always keep the primer application thin. A Hornet after-market head has also been added.

about 30mm of the drill bit protruding from the heel. The drill bit was superglued in place, and acts as the post to prop the figure on a stand. I scrubbed the figure down with an old toothbrush and some vinegar (vinegar works on photo-etch as well) to remove casting agents. I then rinsed off the figure with warm water. I cleaned up any residual casting lines and seams, as described in the *Getting started* chapter.

I temporarily added Warriors resin arms to the figure using Blu-Tack to check suitability and fit. When the placement of the arms appeared correct, I removed the Blu-Tack and added a few drops of superglue between the arms and torso. I applied some car-filler putty with the tip of a hobby blade in the gaps between the shoulder and the torso. Once the putty was applied, I brushed on Tamiya liquid glue over the putty. The glue helps smooth out the putty's rough and gritty edges, and serve as a good alternative to sanding. Once the putty was absolutely dry (20 minutes), the figure was sprayed with two light coats of Tamiya white primer to help show any additional surface flaws and to also provide 'tooth' for subsequent paint.

For base-coating a black uniform, the trick is not to use pure black at the outset, but rather to mix up a warm, dark grey colour. Laying in pure black paint for the base limits your ability to apply subsequent shadows. Therefore, I started with a lighter colour for the base. On my palette, I mixed 80 per cent Humbrol Enamel Matt Black No.33 with 20 per cent Matt Flesh No.61. When using Humbrols, it is best not to shake the tin of paint to mix it. The murky mass that accumulates at the bottom of the tin is ideal for brush painting. I removed a small amount of this chunky mass from the tin with a toothpick, and transferred it to a palette (a simple plastic sheet). I added a few drops of Testors thinner to increase the working time of the paint. The paint was applied to the jacket and trousers using a No.1-sized flat brush, always keeping the brush motion in a vertical and downward direction.

Once the first base layer was dry, I re-applied a second thin coat to the uniform using the same base colour mix, consistency and amount as the first application. This second coat of base paint ensures that all of the white primed areas have been fully covered, and eliminates brush strokes from the first application. As soon as the second coat of paint was applied, I immediately moved to the shading and highlighting process of the uniform.

Shadows and highlights

The shadowing and highlighting of a figure is a critical step, which compensates for the lack of adequate light on a scaled figure. This is particularly evident in a badly lit show room, where the lighting will either be too faint to allow a viewer

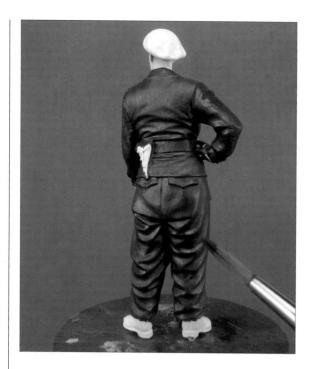

The uniform base mix of 80 per cent Humbrol Enamel Matt Black and 20 per cent Humbrol Enamel Flesh was applied to the whole figure.

As the second base application dries, I immediately moved to the shading process of the uniform. I added 10 per cent Flesh to 90 per cent Flat Black and mixed this up with a large brush and I applied a thin layer of the Medium Shadow paint into all of the folds and recesses.

A close-up view of the shadows added into the folds.

I began the blending process. A clean brush moistened with thinners was lightly jabbed on the border between the base colour and the shadow area.

Note how the shadows appear 'faded in' and the stark shadow border has disappeared. This is the result of blending the paints.

The first highlights were mixed using 30 per cent Flesh to 70 per cent Matt Black on my palette. The highlights were applied on all of the fold tops.

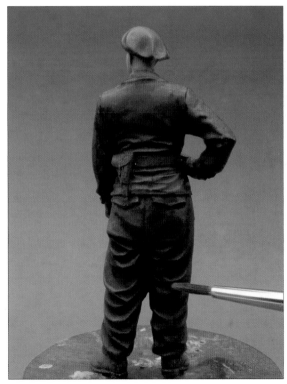

The highlights were blended in by stippling with a finer brush, similar to the application of the shadows.

The second series of highlights was then applied.

The lapels were painted in using Humbrol Matt White. At this point, the head has been painted in oils.

Touch-ups are sometimes necessary, particularly if the highlights are too light. This requires toning them down with a darker shade of the highlight paint. The eyes have also been filled in.

to distinguish details on a figure, or too strong, which washes out any subtle highlights and shadows. Some modellers prefer to apply shadows using a series of washes – similar to washes applied on armour models. While this may work sometimes, there are several other effective, yet risk free, approaches to creating shadows and highlights, and most of the different techniques will be covered in this book.

The technique I have used in this feature begins with two different shadow types – medium shadows and deep shadows. On my palette, I added 10 per cent Matt Flesh to 90 per cent Matt Black and mixed this up with a large brush. I added a little Testors thinner to the mix to thin out the paint. With a No.0 brush, I applied a thin layer of the medium shadow paint into and inside all of the folds and recesses of the trousers and the jacket. If you have trouble identifying the shadow areas, shine a lamp or flashlight directly above the figure to determine where the shadows fall. The medium shadow paint should be placed in any area that looks like a small dip or depression on the surface. On a typical figure, about 50 per cent to 60 per cent of the area being painted will generally take the medium shadow shade.

As soon as the medium shadow was applied, the next step is the blending of the medium shade into the base. At this point, the second base coat is dry, but still workable. Blending the medium shadows into the base requires taking a clean No.1 or No.2 rounded brush moistened with thinner and lightly poking the brush on the border between the semi-dry base colour and the freshly applied wet medium shadow. The small amount of thinner in the brush will loosen up the base paint just enough to blend the freshly applied medium shadow, creating a 'middle' shade that combines the base coat and the medium shadow. This process was applied all of the way around the trousers and jacket.

Next, I moved to the application of the deep shadows. For these I used pure Matt Black with a few drops of Testors thinners to extend the working time of the paint. The deep shadow paint should be added with a small No. 0 pointed brush to the deepest section of the medium shadows and always within the borders of the medium shadow. In very narrow folds, it may only be necessary to paint in a thin line to represent the deep shadow areas. Once the deep shadows were applied, I switched brushes to a clean, thinner-moistened No.1 round brush, and began the task of poking and lightly jabbing the border between the deep shadow and medium shadow. Once the borders between the deep and medium shadows had been blended, I allowed the paint to dry completely overnight.

During the process, a few stumbling blocks may occur. If the paint on your palette starts to dry and becomes thick or lumpy, add a few drops of Testors thinner to extend its working time. Alternatively, you can add a bit of black oil paint to your mix, which will also have the same result. Humbrol enamels are generally quite manageable for 20 to 30 minutes when left exposed. The other option is to make a new batch of paint on your palette. If your brush becomes stiff and hard to work with, switch to a clean, dry brush. It is always useful to have a few brushes handy for this purpose.

After the shadows had been applied, I wanted to apply two highlights – medium highlights and hi-highlights – to the figure's uniform. Some modellers use the dry-brush method to place highlights, and although this can work, it is far more effective to actually paint and blend highlight colours. Dry-brushing is a technique of stroking and rubbing a minimal amount of a lighter-coloured paint on to highlight points. Unfortunately, dry-brushing can leave nasty brush marks, and the action of repeatedly rubbing a brush in a single area can result in the brush hairs polishing the base paint, leaving a glossy or satin finish that cannot be easily remedied with a clear flat overspray.

The technique I use for applying highlights is similar to the shadowing process, with the exception that the colour mixes being applied become lighter in tone, and are applied to the upper surfaces of folds and creases. To make the medium highlights, I mixed a small amount of 30 per cent Matt Flesh with 70 per cent Matt Black on my palette. With a No.0 brush, I applied a thin layer of the medium highlight paint on all of the fold tops of the uniform. The medium highlight paint mix should be placed very sparingly on the top of any area that protrudes from the figure's clothing. On a typical figure, about 30 per cent of the area being painted will generally take the medium highlight paint application.

As soon as the medium highlight paint was applied, I began blending the medium highlight borders. Because the base colour had now fully cured overnight, the blending process of poking and jabbing a brush moistened with thinners on the highlight borders will soften and diffuse the edges of the highlights, rather than actually blending the highlight into the base (which was the case for the shadows). Results may not be apparent at first, but the next step of applying the hi-highlights will begin to show the subtle effect.

I added another 20 per cent Matt Flesh to the medium highlight mix for the hi-highlights. I added a few drops of Testors thinner and applied the paint sparingly on top and within the borders of the medium highlights. Once the hi-highlights were applied, I switched brushes to a clean, thinner-moistened round brush, and began the task of lightly jabbing the border between the semi-wet medium highlights and the freshly applied hi-highlights. This results in the two colours blending and creating a 'middle ground' that combines the two highlight colours. Once I finished the blending process, I allowed the figure to dry thoroughly overnight.

If small mishaps occur along the way, such as shadow paint finding itself on highlight points, just remove the unwanted paint with a few strokes of a thinner-moistened brush. If the highlight points appear too light in tone, mute this down with a slightly darker shade of the highlight. If you note that some

The collar patches are from the Archer Fine Transfers series. I never attempt to rub these down. Instead, I remove the transfer from the carrier with a very sharp hobby knife and apply a little white glue on the back of the transfer.

The completed figure. Note that the piping has been painted in with oil paints.

A close-up of the painted Hornet head.

areas need adjustments and tweaks long after the paint on the figure has dried, make the necessary corrections with minimal amounts of paint, always working in the smallest area at any one time.

In this example, I applied two highlights and two shadows. But it is also possible to apply five or six different shades of each by adding smaller amounts of lighter paint per application for the highlights and smaller amounts of a darker paint for each application of the shadows. It is really up to you to decide what you feel is adequate to attain good results.

The process may seem long and tedious for such subtle effects, but this is the ideal situation – particularly for using black. Understated effects are far more attractive and appealing than overdone effects, and the best way to compare your results is to paint another figure in pure black and compare the two. The results of applying shadows and highlights will quickly become evident.

The most important tip is to take your time when applying the highlights and shadows, and keep the stippling and poking motion light and consistent when blending the borders of each application. The stippling motion can be time-consuming and test your patience, but it is the one step that will make all the difference to your figure's overall appearance.

Painting Afrikakorps Panzer uniforms

Subject:	*Deutsches Afrikakorps Panzertruppen during Rommel's offensive into Egypt, mid-1942*
Modeller/photos:	*Brian Wildfong*
Skill level:	*Advanced*
Base kit:	*Alpine Miniatures resin figure*
Scale:	*1/35*
Paints:	*Winsor & Newton: Ivory Black, Titanium White, Burnt Sienna, Yellow Ochre, Cadmium Red, Permanent Rose Grumbacher: Raw Umber, Burnt Umber Old Holland: Mars Brown*

The Panzertruppen who became part of the famed Deutsches Afrikakorps (DAK) received the same tropical uniform as their comrades in the infantry and artillery. The issue tunic and breeches were manufactured in olive twill, but the harsh desert environment rapidly faded the colour to a variety of shades of tan, khaki and sand. The black Panzer side cap (*Feldmutze*) was typically replaced by the symbol of the DAK, the tropical peaked cap, which the troops bleached to give themselves the look of veteran campaigners. Other characteristic items were the high-laced canvas and leather desert boots. Leather belts were replaced with webbing and metal belt buckles and buttons were sometimes painted green, although the paint quickly wore off. To distinguish the Panzertruppen from other DAK personnel, the tropical tunic retained its pink *Waffenfarbe* piping on the shoulder straps, and the men pinned the silver *Totenkopf* badges from their temperate uniforms to their lapels. Scarves were essential protection from the sun and the *ghibli*, the stinging desert sandstorms that afflicted friend and foe alike.

The Alpine base figure was assembled from stock, checked for seam lines and flash, and then sprayed with two thin coats of aerosol primer to provide a 'tooth' for the colour coats to follow. The figure then received a brushed-on undercoat of acrylic craft paints – Plaid, DecoArt or Delta Ceramcoat are some typical North American labels. They dry to a matt finish, provide a good surface for the oils, and are inexpensive. The acrylic undercoat should be a fairly close match to the desired final colour of the uniform.

The colours were mixed using references as guides and all paints were applied using a size 0 round (pointed) brush for uniform areas such as the tunic and trousers, and smaller size 00 to 5/0 brushes for face, belts, straps and other equipment. The brushes used are made of Taklon, a synthetic fibre. Brian applied several thinned acrylic coats until the coverage was fairly smooth and even.

Even though the figure's tropical tunic and breeches would have been almost identical in colour when first issued, Brian deliberately undercoated them in two slightly different shades of faded khaki, since in the real world, no two articles of clothing fade to the exact same shade. This also helps prevent the figure from looking too monotone.

The tunic and breeches were each undercoated with different combinations of acrylic paints such as Turner's Yellow, Burnt Umber, Raw Umber, Ivory White and Lamp Black, all mixed 'by eye' using colour references. The tropical cap used a

(continues on page 26)

The basic figure in its primer coat. A paper clip in the bottom of the foot attaches it to a 4in. long piece of wood that is stable and comfortable to hold while painting.

Undercoating with acrylics. Note the difference in the colour of the tunic and trousers, as described in the text.

The 'wet-on-wet' process begins. A base coat of Burnt Sienna oils is applied to the face.

A large, dry brush is used to reduce the Burnt Sienna to a thin stain over the undercoat.

Dark shadows being applied to the face with Mars Brown oil colour.

The finished face with light highlights applied and blended. Note the strong contrast between the highlight and shadows.

Blocking in the medium highlight colour prior to blending. The initial medium shadow areas are already blocked in.

Blending the edges of the shadow and highlight areas using a stabbing motion with a clean, dry brush.

Adding secondary highlights along the edge of a pocket. Note the darker outlining and shading already added with Raw Umber.

Outlining the dark scarf/tunic shadow with Raw Umber and a fine pointed brush. These shadows add extra depth to the finished figure and emphasize the equipment.

The breeches and boots with highlights and shadows applied. The glossy reflections will be lost after a sprayed matt coat.

The equipment gets painted wet-on-wet too. The scarf has been painted and the binoculars are being highlighted with grey. The hands have their Burnt Sienna base coat applied, ready for the same shadow and highlight colours as the face.

The completed figure before being sprayed with clear flat. Note how a black oil wash brings out the lace detail on the boots.

After the matt coat. The tiny lettering on the green cuff title was applied with a toothpick splinter.

A good view of the finished boots. Note the dark outlining of the jacket seams and the highlight detail on the pockets.

The belt buckle was painted silver, then given a wash of black oils to tone down the brightness and emphasize detail. Note the trouser shading and highlighting.

similar mix, but with more White to simulate the 'bleached-out' look. Flesh areas were undercoated with a 'warm flesh' mix of White, Burnt Sienna and Turner's Yellow. The eye sockets were painted in a dark grey with a finely pointed 5/0 brush, then trimmed to final eye shape with more of the basic flesh colour.

The real work of bringing a realistic look to the uniform was accomplished by applying and blending oil paints using a technique known as 'wet on wet'. As the name implies, a thin layer of oil paint is applied as a base coat, and then darker shadow and lighter highlight colours are lightly blended into the 'wet' base coat to further emphasize the way the light catches the sculpted details of the figure's uniform and equipment.

Because of their long drying time, oil paints can be worked and blended easily to create very subtle changes in tone. Other colours can also be worked into the oil base coat to create dust, dirt, mud and faded cloth effects; these make a figure appear as though it is living in the environment, rather than just resting on a base.

The first stage in the wet-on-wet process is to create a base coat that has some initial shadows and highlights. The DAK figure had a thin layer of Burnt Sienna oil applied over the whole face, neck and ears. Using a clean, dry (no thinner at all) brush, much of the Burnt Sienna was removed by stroking in a downward motion, leaving a thin stain of 'wet' oil paint on the acrylic undercoat. Shadow areas of the face were then emphasized by applying small amounts of Mars Brown with a finely pointed 5/0 brush to the deep creases of the face (for example, under the eyebrow ridges and under the jaw line). A highlight colour was mixed from Burnt Sienna and White, and this was then applied to the parts of the face that would catch the light shining down from above (the eyebrow ridges, bridge of the nose, cheekbones, etc.).

Using a light, up-and-down stabbing motion with the point of a brush, the highlight colours can be subtly blended into the still-wet Burnt Sienna base coat (hence the name 'wet on wet'). This process should be done with a very dry paintbrush. It is well worth having a few brushes on hand and an old rag to wipe and remove excess paint from the bristles on your brushes.

To paint the figure's faded tunic and breeches, Brian used a slight variation of the wet-on-wet technique. Instead of applying a stain coat of a single colour as a base, he blocked in areas of medium shadow and highlight colours, then blended them together along their edges to produce a base coat with some subtle shadows, highlights and mottling.

For the tunic, Brian mixed a medium shadow using Burnt Umber, Gold Ochre, Titanium White and a touch of Black to produce a brownish khaki colour. This was applied in a very thin layer to the shadow areas of the tunic; for example, under the pocket flaps, below the folds and in wrinkles on the sleeves. A highlight made from the same colours as the shadow, but with less Burnt Umber, was then applied as a very thin layer to the raised areas on the tops of folds, edges of pockets and coat tails.

Next, a size 0 dry brush was gently stabbed or jabbed at the boundary between the blocks of shadow and highlight, lightly blending the two colours together only along their edges. This keeps some of the shadow colour in the shadow areas and the highlight colour in the highlight areas, but reduces the contrast between them, creating a subtle, gradual transition between light and dark. A handy rule of thumb is to stop blending a bit earlier than you think you should. Resist the temptation to blend all the shadow and highlight areas together into one solid mass of the same colour. At the end of the blending, you should still be able to see the difference in colour between the shadow and highlight areas.

Once the initial blending was done, Brian went back and deepened the tone of some of the shadow areas by blending straight Burnt Umber into them. Brian also used it to outline the uniform's seams, pockets, collar and shoulder straps using a finely pointed 5/0 brush. More White was added to the highlight

The completed figure, posed on unpainted groundwork, with a scissors telescope and tripod from the spare parts box. The telescope helps to give the figure some context, but keep these 'props' small in number in a single figure display like this.

colour and then blended along the edges of the pockets, tops of seam lines and the tops of some of the folds, again with a 5/0 brush point and a very light blending motion. The breeches then received the same wet-on-wet treatment as the tunic, except that he used Raw Umber instead of Burnt Umber in the khaki mix to keep some variation between the two pieces of the uniform.

At this point, the figure was set aside to let the oils dry (usually about 24 hours). After this, the uniform colours typically look slightly glossy. This will be eliminated at the end of painting process with an overall spray of a clear matt. The figure was inspected under different light sources, and the shadows and highlights were fine tuned. For example, the deep fold at the elbow of the left arm received a deeper shadow by adding Ivory Black.

The completed figure with a photo of a desert in the background.

The boots required a couple of different techniques. The tall canvas uppers were shadowed and highlighted wet-on-wet using Ivory Black mixed with Gold Ochre to make an olive green base coat, with shadows created by blending in more Black, and highlights with more Gold Ochre mixed with White. Once dry, Brian used a light brown (Burnt Umber mixed with Titanium White) and the side of a 5/0 brush to lightly touch this colour onto the laces. Once the laces had dried, a wash of Ivory Black and mineral (a.k.a. white) spirit was applied around the laces to bring these out from the olive background colour. The leather parts of the boots were undercoated with Burnt Sienna and base-coated with Burnt Umber, most of which was wiped off with a clean, dry brush. Shadows were added wet-on-wet with Raw Umber, and highlights from

Burnt Sienna mixed with White, well blended into the base coat for a dusty, worn look.

Finally, the smaller detail items were painted using the fine point of a 5/0 brush. The binoculars were undercoated in a dark grey acrylic, and base-coated with dark grey oils (Ivory Black mixed with Titanium White). Shadows were done with Ivory Black, and highlights added with the grey base mix plus more White, again blended wet-on-wet. The pistol holster was treated similarly, but with Burnt Sienna added to the highlight colour for a worn-leather look along the edges.

Metal items, such as the belt buckle, buttons, the lapel skulls and the Panzer Assault Badge, were base coated with acrylic silver. This, however, was too bright for a 1/35-scale figure, so the details were brought out, and the brightness of the silver toned down, with a wash of Ivory Black oil paint.

Insignia such as the breast and cap eagle badges and the shoulder straps were undercoated in a blue/grey acrylic mix, then washed with a darker grey to accentuate details. The pink piping on the shoulder straps and field cap were painted in Permanent Rose oil colour. Brian used oils so that if he botched these fine lines, they could be removed with a brush moistened with white spirit.

The very small details, such as the black, white and red cockade in the centre of the field cap, the white lettering on the green 'AFRIKAKORPS' cuff title and the whites of the figure's eyes, were spotted in using the tip of a splintered toothpick. As a final touch, and only after the figure had dried thoroughly (three to four days), the figure was sprayed with two coats of a clear matt applied by spray can (Testors Dullcote). This protects the paint job and eliminates any 'glossies' left behind as a result of the wet-on-wet blending technique.

Making a base for your DAK figure

The groundwork being applied. The grey material in the bowl is Celluclay papier-mâché mixed with water and white glue so it sticks better.

The base is a piece of 2in. x 2in. basswood, stained in red mahogany and sealed with clear gloss polyurethane.

After the Celluclay is applied and smoothed out, gutter gravel is sprinkled on and tamped in. The hole for the figure's location is marked with a toothpick.

The finished base before painting in various sandy tones. Brian used acrylic base coats with oil washes and dry-brushing to simulate the dusty desert floor.

The pin in the figure's boot sole is inserted into the marked hole.

The figure is gently pushed into its permanent position.

Painting the Sturmartillerie two-piece denim

Subject:	*Sturmartillerie (Assault Artillery)*
Modeller/photos:	*Denis Allaire*
Skill level:	*Advanced*
Base kit:	*Alpine Miniatures, resin*
Scale:	*1/35*
Paints:	*Humbrol Enamel Matt Beige Green*
	Delta Ceramcoat Seminole Green and Black
	Holbein oil paints: Titanium White, Yellow Ochre,
	Payne's Gray, Burnt Sienna, Ultramarine Blue, Burnt
	Umber, Lamp Black, Raw Umber

In early 1942, a new two-piece, reed-green denim suit, almost identical in cut to the black uniform, was issued to tank crews. Each batch was slightly different in colour, but the most common detail was a large pocket on the left breast, either in a vertical position or slightly slanted inwards. The trousers had a distinctive large pocket on the left thigh just above the knee. The rank patches, shoulder straps, collar patches and breast eagle were all applied to this suit.

Denis Allaire is an award-winning figure painter from Quebec City who is primarily a modeller of Napoleonic and medieval subjects, where high contrasts between shadows and highlights are desirable to show quality of texture and fabric. Using his technique to achieve high contrasts in hues and colour tones, he chose to paint a 1/35-scale Alpine Miniatures Panzer crewman to demonstrate a different approach to painting figures using oils. His technique calls for more light and dark colours added to the base, to further accentuate highlights and shadows.

Denis started by priming the figure in Humbrol Enamel Matt Beige Green No.90 to help show any surface flaws. Because the figure was designed to fit inside a turret, he decided to alter the left arm to suggest that the figure was lifting an object – in this case, a jerry can. The conversion of the left arm was made using Milliput Standard Epoxy Putty applied in small pieces under the left armpit. Once the appropriate amount of epoxy was in place to fill gaps, he used a wet, round synthetic brush to sculpt and shape the putty. With a hobby knife, further creases and folds were also worked into the wet putty.

Once the Matt Beige Green 'primer' and putty were dry, Denis applied one light brush application of acrylic Delta Ceramcoat Green mixed with water to provide a light base to work from.

Denis started with the flesh tones by mixing on his palette a combination of Titanium White and Burnt Sienna oil paints in a 7:1 ratio. He also added a speck of Ultramarine Blue to the mix. This flesh base mix was divided into six separate samples on his palette, each about the size of a thumbnail. Three of these samples (A, B, C) would be used for the shadows and two (D, E) for the highlights. The sixth sample (F) would remain as the base flesh. For the shadows, he added 20 per cent Burnt Sienna to A, 40 per cent of Burnt Sienna to B and 30 per cent Burnt Umber to C (for the deepest shadows). For

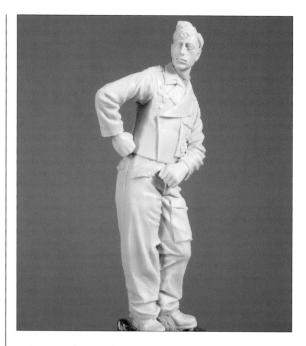

TOP Alpine Miniatures' 1/35-scale resin Sturmartillerie figure.

ABOVE The small modification to the left arm was made using Milliput Standard Epoxy Putty and a wet rounded synthetic brush to sculpt and shape the putty into place.

highlights, he added 20 per cent Titanium White to D and 40 per cent Titanium White to E.

The base colour (F) was applied to the whole face very thinly – just enough to cover the surface. Denis then began working in the various shades of shadows, going from dark to darker (A – B – C respectively) by stippling the border between the flesh base and shadows. While the shadow paints were still wet, he then worked in the two highlight colours (D, E), blending the colours with a light jabbing motion of his brush. The process for painting a face is mostly about analyzing the figure under a light to determine where the highlights and shadows should fall. It is a step that will eventually come naturally, and studying other modellers' treatment of faces is an excellent way to learn.

For the uniform, Denis applied a thin layer of acrylics using Ceramcoat Seminole Green 02422 and Black 02506. Once the base acrylic paint had dried, he started by mixing Titanium White, Payne's Gray, Yellow Ochre and Olive Green oil paints in a 2:2:2:5 ratio. This was applied thinly on the figure's jacket, and all excess oil paint was removed by lightly dragging a large, round brush all the way around the figure.

For the shadows, Denis added 20 per cent Payne's Gray and began the process of stippling and jabbing the shadow paints into all of the folds and creases, and any area on the surface that looked like a depression. This included adding thin lines of the shadow into and along pocket flaps and seams. An additional 15 per cent Payne's Gray was added to the mix, and further paint was applied into the very deepest recesses on the uniform. Once all of the shadows were added, Denis began the stippling action with a dry, round brush, blending the border of the shadows with the base colour of the uniform. As a last step, a large, rounded brush was lightly flicked in a downward motion all the way around the figure to remove excess paint, and also blend the shades further.

As soon as the shadows were blended, he then started the first set of highlights, adding 15 per cent Titanium White to the uniform base colour on his palette. The first highlights were added to all protruding areas of the uniform. Most of the highlights were thin lines of paint applied directly onto the surface, then blended into the surrounding colours with a dry brush. A second highlight was added using 20 per cent more Titanium White to the previous highlight mix, and this was selectively applied to the most protruding areas on the uniform.

The last step was once again lightly dragging a large, dry, round brush in a downward motion around the figure to remove excess paint and further blend the colours. The figure was then set inside an overturned drinking glass on top of a radiator to dry for a week. Once the uniform was completely dry, various touch-ups were made by adding further shadows and highlights where necessary, or in areas that were missed the first time.

The boots were painted in a mix of Lamp Black mixed with Raw Umber oil paints in a 50:50 mix. Once the dark paint was applied, Denis then used some of the flesh colours on his palette for the face and hands, and stippled this into the boots to show wear and tear. To finish off the figure, all details on the uniform were applied with an 0 brush and oil paints.

The base was applied thinly on the entire figure's uniform.

The first application of shadows in all of the creases of the figure.

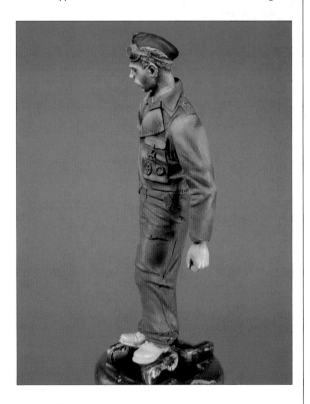

The jacket has two shadows applied and one set of highlights. Note the contrast to the trousers, which have only received a base coat.

A second highlight has been applied to the jacket.

For the shadows, Denis added 20 per cent Payne's Gray and began the process of stippling and jabbing the shadow paints into all the folds and creases.

The first shadows have been blended into the base of the trousers.

A second shadow with 15 per cent more Payne's Gray was applied into the very deepest recesses on the uniform.

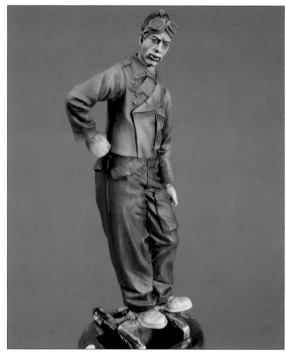

Note the contrast between the jacket (that has one set of highlights) and the trousers (which only have shadows).

The last set of shadows added on the trousers.

The stippling action with a dry rounded brush, blending the border of the shadows with the base colour of the uniform.

A set of highlights applied on the trousers by adding 15 per cent Titanium White to the uniform base-colour.

After a second highlight was added using 20 per cent more White to the previous highlight mix, the stippling motion blended all of the borders of the various tones of colours.

RIGHT The completed figure.

BELOW The figure next to an
SdKfz 233 on a simple base.

Sculpting a Panzer crewman figure

Subject:	*Panzertruppen, Eastern Front*
Modeller/photos:	*Taesung Harmms*
Skill level:	*Master*
Scale:	*1/35*
Additional materials used:	*Brass wires, A&B putty, Evergreen sheet styrene, hobby knives*

Taesung Harmms is the creator of some of the finest resin figures on the market, under the label of Alpine Miniatures. In sculpting and scratch-building figures, Taesung starts by studying photos in books and references. When he finds an appropriate subject, he starts a series of 1/35-scale sketches in different views and angles to help better visualize the finished figure. These sketches and initial plans will go through some small modifications as sculpting progresses.

For tools, Taesung uses brass wire in various diameters, connected to styrene tubes. The tips of the brass rods are filed to different shapes to suit different tasks. The putty used to build the figure is normally the A&B mixing type in solid white. Freshly mixed putty tends to stick to the brass tips, so first they are dipped in baby oil. Regular No.11 hobby blades are used extensively for carving, shaving and making seams in the uniforms. Better tools lead to better results.

The first step in the construction of a figure is developing an armature. It is probably the most important stage because it forms the skeleton on which to work. Because the armature is made of brass wire, the pose can easily be altered to achieve the correct stance. The realism of a figure is more about the position and pose, and less about the fine surface details.

In 1/35 scale, a man standing 5ft 11in. (approximately 180cm) translates into 51mm from the bottom of the feet to the top of the head. Keeping this in mind, Taesung starts the armature by connecting two small pieces of resin blocks with brass wires. One resin block represents the middle torso and ribcage, and the other block represents the pelvis. He then connects two brass wires to make the legs, and bends the wire to the correct position for the knees. In making these bends, other parts of the body also need to be altered, such as the lower back, the hips and the ankles. It is better to slightly exaggerate certain characteristics in a pose to avoid a figure appearing too static. To assist you in achieving realistic poses, make frequent reference to photos of humans in various stances to capture the overall position of the limbs, torso, hips and feet.

Once the armature is complete, the next step is fleshing out the armature and capturing the figure's proportions. Taesung adds A&B putty to the armature to build up a first layer that represents the human body. Again, looking through photos and images will help immensely. With the addition of a layer of putty over the armature, the figure begins to take shape. In this stage, small amounts of putty are added or removed to bring balance and correctly proportion the figure. Once the armature has been covered with a layer of putty, it is important that the overall appearance is on the 'lean' side to allow room for the clothing.

With all of the tools and reference materials in hand, Taesung starts on the uniform. He usually starts from the bottom and works his way to the top,

RIGHT AND BELOW The sculpting tools and scalpels that Taesung uses when scratchbuilding his figures.

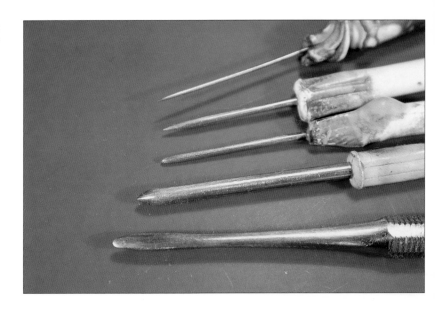

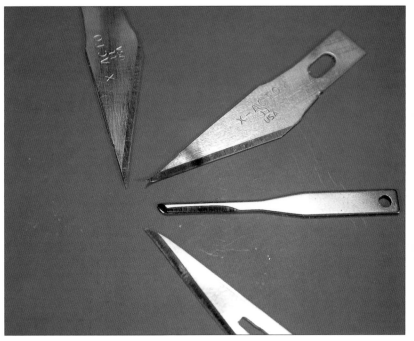

always working from inside to outside. His initial sketches come in handy and help him plan ahead.

The first clothing step in this case was the winter boots. The lower parts of the boots are carved from resin blocks. Putty is then added to the ankles and lower legs. Wrinkles at the ankles and the top of the feet are made to represent worn leather. An old, stiff brush is used to make the rough hide on the boots by lightly jabbing the brush onto the semi-wet putty.

For the winter trousers, Taesung was extra careful making the fabric folds and wrinkles, because these are very prominent on the figure. Again, to make the folds look natural, it is essential to have good references. Also, it is important to keep in mind that different fabrics show different types of wrinkles. Based on wartime photos, this type of trouser had a distinctive baggy look, with large, round wrinkles. Because the putty has a one-hour working

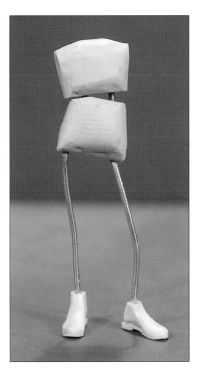

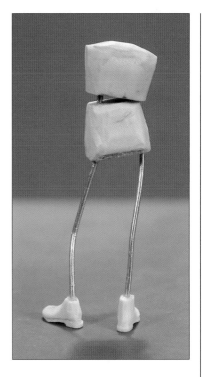

The first step in the construction of a figure is developing an armature from brass wire and two small pieces of resin blocks.

The brass wire is bent to shape.

Note how the right hip is counter-balanced by a bent left knee.

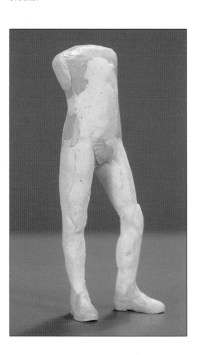

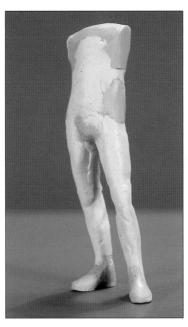

Once the armature is complete, the next step is fleshing out the armature and capturing proportion.

Taesung added A&B putty to the armature to build up a first layer that represents the human body.

The lower parts of the boots were carved out of resin blocks and putty was then added to the ankles and lower legs. A stiff brush was used to make the rough hide part of the boots.

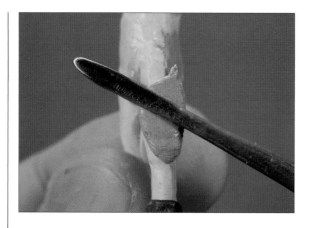

Taesung applied A&B putty to create the trousers and shaped the folds and creases with his fingers.

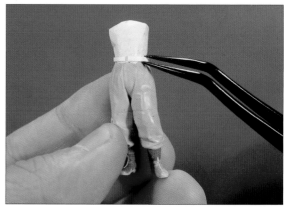

The belt was made from a thin strip of sheet styrene and applied to the figure.

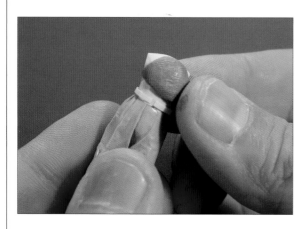

Putty was spread out over the upper body to represent the jacket.

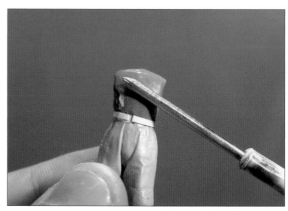

The putty was then thinned out and worked with various tools to create folds and surface details.

Adding the folds to the wet putty. The head has been added temporarily.

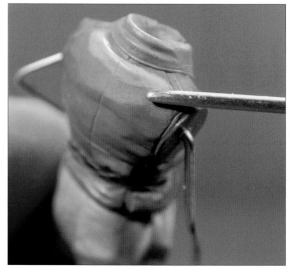

Creating the wrinkles and folds. The collar has been added now too.

time, Taesung worked on one leg at a time. Most of the detail is done while the putty is wet. Once the putty has dried, small alterations and modifications can be made, either by adding more putty in very thin layers, or shaving putty off with a blade.

Once the trousers were completed and dried, it was time to start the Russian belt. The belt was made before the jacket because the manner in which the belt is worn dictates the wrinkles around the waist of the jacket. A thin strip of sheet styrene was used to make the belt. Though the belt was issued to Russian army officers, it was also popular with German officers. This type of belt also had elaborate stitching, and Taesung simulated the stitching by scribing the details into the styrene with a sharp brass rod. A holster for a P38 was carved entirely out of a piece of resin, except for the strap that holds down the holster cover.

The sheepskin jacket was not a common piece of clothing, but was issued to army and Waffen-SS troops in small numbers. These jackets varied in details and quality, but appear to have had a certain basic design. During the German invasion of France, French army motorcycle riders wore animal-skin jackets that were almost identical. Although some officers were photographed in modified versions, most jackets appear to have the following characteristics: tight fitting, no collar, single breasted with five buttons and hoops, open cuffs, short waist, and seams reinforced with thin strips of fabric. Again, studying photos is important to portray a convincing leather jacket. Leather has folds and wrinkles distinctive from wool or cotton. Taesung sculpted the front and back of the jacket in one sitting, and while the putty was still workable, he pushed a pair of binoculars into the chest to make a natural indentation in the jacket.

Explaining the intricacies of sculpting a head warrants a manual of its own. However, in brief, the head was modified from an earlier one that Taesung had sculpted. He shaved off some of the features, and new features were added on the nose and cheeks. The head was attached to the body with a short brass rod running through the middle of the neck. Careful positioning of the head is an important step to help give the figure a natural look and some 'attitude'. The position of the head will inevitably determine the overall appearance of the figure. Once the head was positioned, Taesung added putty around the neck to make the collar of a shirt and Panzer jacket. Before he added wet putty around the neck, baby oil was applied at the bottom of the neck to keep the head from sticking to the torso. Keeping the head separate makes the painting process much easier.

Making realistic hands is probably the most difficult part of sculpting a human form. Taesung finds it easier to carve and shave a solid resin block than to work from 'scratch' with soft putty. Instead of working on small details at a time, he gets the basic shape and size from the resin block, then gradually shapes the whole hand by snipping off bits.

The next step is adding the arms. Taesung drilled a hole in the torso on each side and inserted a brass rod. Once he had bent the brass rod into the appropriate pose, the hands were added. Getting the right arm length can be slightly tricky, particularly when they are bent at the elbow. Before putty is added to flesh out the arms, Taesung places some baby oil on the torso so that the arm does not stick to the torso while the putty dries. Once the putty hardens, more putty is added to make the sleeves. Bent arms have more severe folds and wrinkles than straight arms. Like the details on the trousers, extra attention must be paid to the sleeves to capture realistic folds and wrinkles.

With the figure almost complete, it was time to add the smaller details, such as insignia and buttons. Also, careful inspection of the figure under intense lighting is important to help locate areas that were missed or need to be touched up. Rough surface areas can easily be sanded down with fine sandpaper or shaved off with a sharp blade. Once the figure was thoroughly dry, it was cast in resin and was ready for painting.

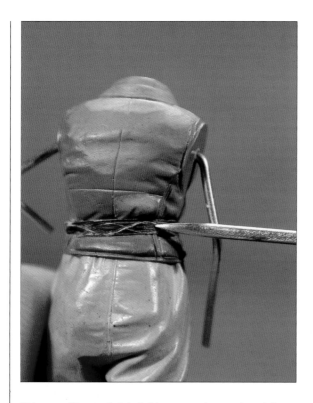

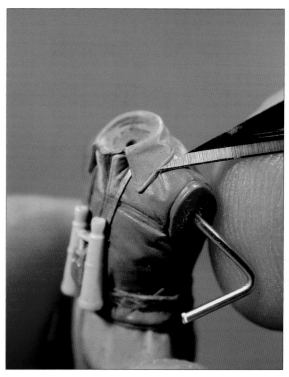

This type of Russian belt had elaborate stitching work, and this was added by scribing the details into the styrene with a sharp brass rod.

The end of a hobby knife blade was used to carve and scribe details on the lapels of the jacket.

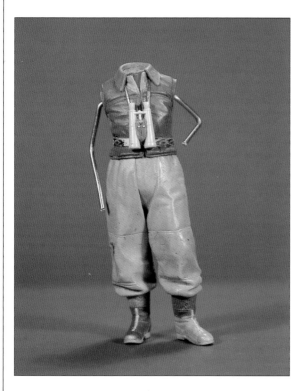

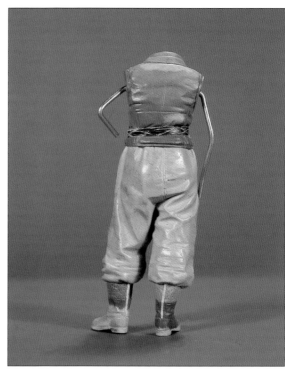

A front view of the figure, showing the binoculars in place.

A rear view of the figure.

The arms are in the process of being fleshed out now.

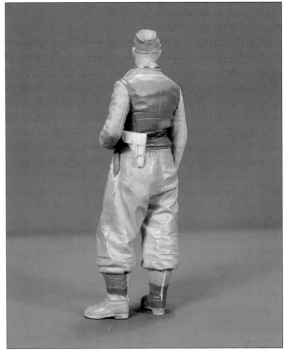

The arms have been completed; particular attention has been placed on achieving realistic folds and wrinkles in the elbow area.

A close-up of the upper torso. Note the addition of the insignia and buttons.

The completed figure ready for casting.

Making hands from resin blocks

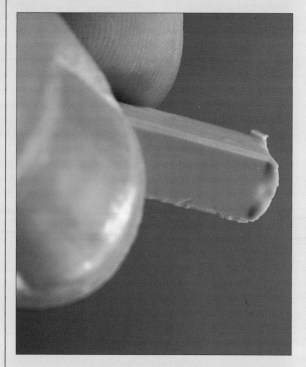

Taesung starts with a solid piece of resin.

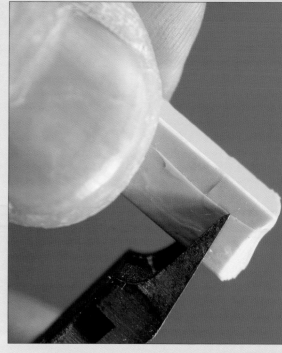

He then snips off parts to approximately the correct size.

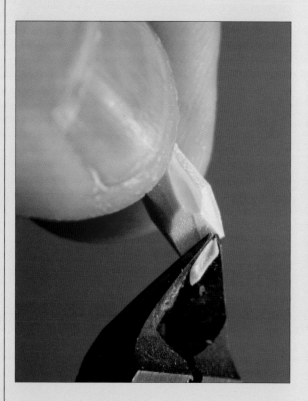

He then carves and shaves bits of resin from the block, until he gets the basic shape and size.

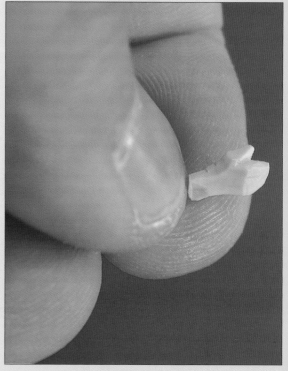

The shape of the hand is complete. It now requires some fine sanding and carving into the resin for the final result.

Painting small-scale Panzer figures (1/48)

Subject:	*Sturmartillerie, Italy, 1943*
Modeller/photos:	*Garfield Ingram*
Skill level:	*Advanced*
Base kit:	*Mike Good*
Scale:	*1/48*
Paints:	*Citadel White primer. Humbrol Enamel: Matt Black, Matt Flesh, Matt White, Red Brown, Matt Leather, Matt Uniform Grey, Matt Field Grey.*

In recent years, there has been an explosion of kits released in 1/48 scale. With this revival of quarter scale has come a renewed interest in 1/48-scale figures. While older releases in this scale by Bandai, Dartmoor and Hecker & Goros were adequate, recent releases by Tamiya and Skybow have brought about major changes in both quantity and quality.

Garfield Ingram, a well-known Canadian modeller in 1/48 scale and creator of Track48, kindly agreed to share his approach to painting such figures in this chapter. All of the techniques that Garfield uses have been learned from those who work in larger scales, with some added tweaks and modifications.

As with larger figures, good brushes, bright lighting and patience are the basic requirements for satisfying results. Perhaps the most important advice is to start off with a quality figure. Faces must be believable, clothing folds should be well articulated, and the pose and gestures should be interesting. Therefore, precision is of the highest importance when painting a face, to ensure symmetry and believable colouring. The first step is to clean up the figure.

Whether it be injection-moulded plastic or a hand-cast resin piece, there will be mould seams to remove. Garfield uses a combination of scraping with a No.11 X-Acto blade and fine sandpaper to achieve this. Priming the figure is also an essential step, and he prefers to use Gunze Mr. Surfacer. A primer is an essential 'tool,' particularly for small figures, because seams and surface flaws are much more difficult to identify at this size.

In general, primer is best sprayed on. Brushing on primers can leave brush marks, which are difficult to address once painting begins. Aim for a smooth, controlled surface. Another benefit to spraying is that it takes less primer to cover the surface. Hand painting will tend to fill in and obliterate sharply defined details. This applies to the major areas of the face and clothing.

To fill in gaps and voids on the surface, Garfield uses standard Squadron Putty. This product does not stick to white metal or resin, but it adheres well to areas that have been primed. Once the filling and sanding of the blemishes is complete, another thin coat of primer is applied to seal the filler and give the figure an even surface, especially with respect to absorbency.

The face is the most important area of the figure, and if painted well, it will establish the degree of success of the final product. When painting a face, it is best to keep it simple and avoid trying to make the figure frown or smile.

Garfield uses a range of Humbrol enamels, such as Matt Flesh No.61, Matt Leather No.62 and Red Brown No.160. The range of values of these colours is regularly spaced from very light to dark.

To start the face, a coat of Matt Flesh was applied as a base, ensuring that the paint was neither too thick nor too thin. Having a small cup of paint thinner

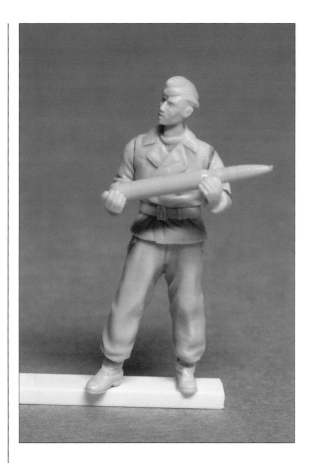

The subject is a re-loading Tiger crew by Mike Good. This set was moulded in resin and comes with three figures passing 88 rounds along.

Garfield sprayed a coat of Mr. Surfacer to seal the surface, create a neutral base, and to help locate surface imperfections.

to hand is useful for making adjustments to the consistency. It is imperative that the first coat is allowed to dry for 24 hours, as it is going to take a considerable beating.

The recesses and shadow areas of the face were then painted with a 50:50 mixture of Matt Flesh and Matt Leather using a fine brush. This coat is a bit thinner than the one used for the base coat. When this application was dry (in a few minutes), the edges were blended into the base colour using fresh paint thinner and a fine brush. When this stage is finished, there should be only the slightest shift in value seen on the face. In other words, the sharp border between the base and the freshly applied shadows should be blended out.

Using some thinned Matt Flesh, the deep recesses were then painted, making sure that the area covered was smaller than the previous one. Again, this was blended with a small brush and paint thinner. The last stage was to apply Red and blend the very deepest recesses – under the chin, eyes and behind the ears. On the tops of the cheeks, tip of the nose, lips and above the eyebrows, Garfield finished off with a very light mix of Matt White No.34, Matt Flesh, and a touch of Red Brown. This will create a healthy-looking highlight, but be careful not to overdo it.

The eyes and eyebrows should be painted using a fine, tapered brush. A fine line is all that is required for the eyes, because at this scale, it is virtually impossible to see them. Both the eyebrows and the eyes should be made of lines that taper to a point at the outside ends. When complete, it may be necessary to pick out very small areas, such as the line of the mouth and inside

After the first coat of Mr. Surfacer, imperfections are corrected and the joints between the arms have been filled and smoothed down.

Mr. Surfacer was used to rebuild the seam that was lost when blending the arm in. A strip of tape was applied to define the location of the seam. Once the Mr. Surfacer was dry, the joints were sanded to smooth out ridges.

the ear and nostrils, with a very dark brown to sharpen up the details. Hair can be painted by applying dark brown, followed by at least two layers of light browns to create highlights.

After the face and sidecap were complete, Garfield painted the tunic with Humbrol Matt Uniform Grey No.111. He allowed the tunic to dry for 24 hours because the subsequent treatment involved considerable thinners. A mix of thinned Matt Uniform Grey and Matt Black No.33 was added to create the shadow areas. The paint was applied in narrow swathes in the recesses of the folds. As soon as it was dry, Garfield used a thinner-moistened brush to blend the edges of the shadows into the base colour with short, jabbing strokes.

An even darker grey was mixed up with more Matt Black, which was then painted into the very deepest recesses of the folds. Again, this thin coat was blended into the adjacent mid-shadows, always ensuring a smooth transition between the two colours. Pure Matt Black was applied to the darkest recesses, such as the inside edges of the fly, pockets, etc. This step helps accentuate the edges of the deepest recessed lines.

For the highlights, Matt Field Grey was mixed with Matt White. This mixture should be lighter than the original base colour. This was applied to the upper edges of the folds, and only allowed to dry for a few minutes, then blended into the surrounding area. If needed, Garfield also applies an even lighter grey to the very tops of the folds, collar and pockets.

The same technique was used when painting the black trousers. The base colour used was pure Matt Black. A series of dark grey tones were applied to bring out the tops of the folds.

One last light coat of primer was applied to seal the filler and created an even and smooth surface.

The face and hands were painted with a base of Humbrol Matt Flesh No.61. After this had dried for 48 hours, a thinned mixture of Humbrol 61 mixed with 62 was applied to the recesses of the face and hands.

A small brush moistened with paint thinner was stippled on to soften the edges of the darker areas.

At this stage, the deepest recesses of the face have been painted and blended with Humbrol 160. The eyes were painted using No.170 but the whites and irises were not applied. At this scale, a very dark line will suffice.

Highlights were applied using a reddish hue to the high spots on the face such as the cheeks and forehead. The careful blending process was repeated.

The side cap and collar were painted in using Humbrol paints.

The base colour of the tunic was applied using Humbrol No.111. When the base coat was thoroughly dried and cured, the recesses were painted in with a 50:50 mixture of No.111 and Matt Black.

A mixture of very dark grey was applied to the folds.

The final blending and stippling of the grey on the trousers provides a nice subtle highlight.

The completed figure next to a DML 1/35-scale figure.

Special techniques

Painting flesh and faces

Subject:	*Paiting Panzertruppen flesh and faces*
Modeller:	*Mark Bannerman*
Base kit:	*Hornet 1/35-scale resin heads*
Paints:	*Citadel White primer*
	Rembrandt: Gold Ochre
	Van Gogh: Titanium White
	Winsor & Newton: Burnt Sienna
	Winton: Burnt & Raw Umber

I will alternatively paint a head in enamels or in oils – or in a combination of both mediums. I tend to believe that oil paints are probably the easiest of the two types for painting flesh tones, for several reasons. Oil paints are vivid, manageable and easily altered. The best feature is that oil paints have a long drying time, which allows for ample time to make corrections. Taking my time and working in 10–15-minute sessions per day is a most agreeable way to conduct my favourite hobby!

Oil paints

To paint flesh, I typically mix three oil colours – Gold Ochre, Burnt Sienna and Titanium White – in a 2:1:4 ratio. However, there are many other variations of mixes depending on your tastes. These can include Zinc White mixed with Raw Sienna and Brown Madder; or Flake White, Yellow Ochre and Van Dyke Brown; or Transparent White, Naples Yellow and Mars Violet Deep. Any combination of the aforementioned whites, yellows and browns should provide very satisfactory results. It is really a question of experimenting. As a small note, wet oil paints tend to dry to a slightly darker shade, so be generous when adding the white oil paint.

Oil mediums

I will sometimes add a small amount of Winsor & Newton Liquin to my oil flesh paint mix (about 10 per cent). Liquin is a medium that helps oil paints dry to a satin finish, improves the flow of oil colours and also speeds up drying time. But Liquin is not absolutely necessary, an acrylic clear gloss coat sprayed on the figure's head after the flesh paint dries is just as effective. Alternatively, I will carefully apply a mixture of rubbing alcohol and a clear gloss by brush to high points on the face – above eyebrows, on the cheekbones, nose bridge and nostrils, tips of ears, and in the middle of the lower lip. This will accentuate the highlights, resulting in greater depth to your flesh tone.

Painting eyes

The eyes will always be the focus of any diorama or vignette: two tiny specks on a comparatively massive diorama will draw the viewer's attention immediately. To alleviate any apprehensions you may have about this step, it is really not too onerous. Remember that if you mess up the eyes – not straight, too big, or the dreaded 'pop-eyed' look – just pick out the paint in the problem

(continues on page 57)

For my subject, I used one of the after-market resin heads from the excellent Hornet series.

I primed the head in Citadel primers (white) with two light coats.

I airbrushed a base in an off-white creamy colour. I generally use acrylics for the base with a Tamiya Desert Yellow mixed with Flat White in a ratio of 1:8. Another alternative is Humbrol Flesh mixed with Matt White in a 1:4 ratio.

I applied a wash of Burnt Umber oil paints mixed with Testors thinners. The wash should be tinted thinners (and not thinned paint) and I apply this wash to the entire face and neck.

If the wash is too heavy, I usually dab a small fine brush on the face and the bristles will soak up any excess thinner. I try not to fiddle too much as the wash may lift the undercoat. Best to start with small amounts of wash, let it dry, and add more as you see fit.

To paint flesh, I mix three oil colours – Gold Ochre, Burnt Sienna and Titanium White – in a 2:1:4 ratio. This is applied in a very thin coat to the face and spread out.

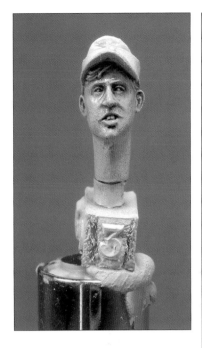

When applying the flesh paint, I avoid as much as possible painting in the eye-sockets or directly placing the paint on top of the original wash of Burnt Umber.

Another thinly spread coat of the same Flesh oil paint was spread out over the face surface. The paint has to be so thin that you should still be able to see the underlying base coat.

I allowed this to dry for two hours under direct light. The paint is still quite wet and this is favourable for the next step.

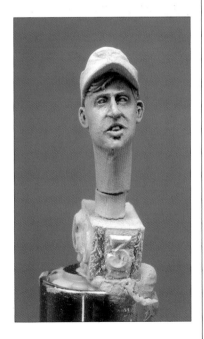

The next step was adding the highlights. With the aid of a toothpick, I added a small amount of white oil to the highlight points. The primary highlight points include upper cheekbones and the ridge of the nose.

With a large rounded brush, I very lightly stippled and poked the brush in a downward motion. The white paint is blended into the semi-dry flesh colours leaving a subtle highlight colour.

The effects of the highlight will not be apparent while the paint is wet. Oil paints are generally glossy when wet and obliterate the highlights completely. However, as it dries, one will begin to see the results.

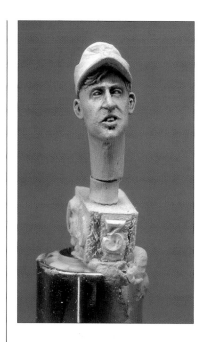

For the lips, I only paint the lower lip. Generally, the best combination for lip colour is to take the base flesh colour (i.e. Gold Ochre, White and Burnt Sienna) and mix with either a dash of Alizarin Crimson oils or Humbrol Wine in a 50:50 ratio.

The figure's hat is base-painted in a mix of Humbrol Black and Matt Flesh.

Sometimes painting a head piece or hat while painting flesh can help better determine if the flesh tones are correct and complementary.

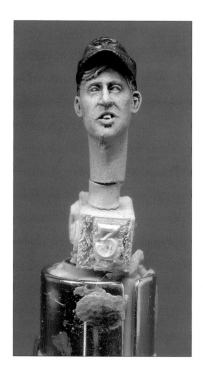

Rosy cheeks are easily duplicated by adding Burnt Sienna to the flesh base in a 1:1 ratio and lightly applying the Sienna in a stippling motion to the cheek areas.

It is best to apply this rosy effect when the base flesh tone used for the face is still wet so that you can blend the two together.

I have kept the rosy cheeks very subtle although one could optionally make the cheeks far more pronounced by adding more Sienna.

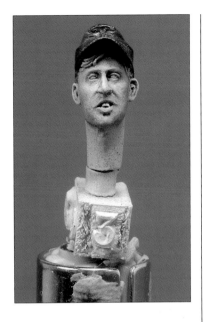

For the beard growth, I prefer using a combination of Payne's Gray oil paint with Raw Umber and applying it very lightly to the beard area in a stippling motion.

Another highlight of white was added using the same technique as described earlier but with slightly less paint.

Highlights were blended carefully in a stippling motion into the Burnt Sienna at the top of the cheeks.

For the eyeballs, a speck of Humbrol 'Flesh' is mixed into white oil paint and then applied to the eyeball area with a toothpick splinter.

Both eyeballs have received the white treatment. I also added in eyebrows as these provide considerable character to the figure and help accentuate the eyes further. I used a toothpick splinter to apply a thin line of Raw Umber oil paints across the eyebrow area.

To paint the irises, I use the very same technique as I did to apply the whites of the eyes. In adding the irises, I avoid straight head-on stares and generally I place irises looking slightly off-centre – either looking left or right. I mixed some Lamp Black and Raw Umber oil paints and placed a speck in each of the corners of the eye sockets. It is virtually impossible to control the shape of the irises, but ensure that the irises cover about 70 per cent of the entire eye socket.

ABOVE The figure's dirty trousers and sweater were created using enamels and by stippling and blending the paint into the base colours. The Academy Tiger I in the background is by Chris Roy.

socket with the end of a splintered toothpick (literally scrape it out) and try again. If you are right-handed, generally the right eye will turn out fine – the left eye will be your problem eye. I would suggest leaving one eye as a reference and only correct the other, as opposed to trying to fix both. If the dark colour for the iris is overlapping the lid, or too much white was dabbed on, just remove it with a scrape of a toothpick. Keep at this until you are satisfied with the eyes – it just takes patience and time.

Painting hands

I treat these similarly to the face. However, the Raw Umber wash could be a little heavier to ensure that the recesses between the fingers are accentuated. Another wash of Burnt Sienna will shade those areas between the deep shadows and high points on the hand. A neat trick after this all dries is to add little specks of white oil on the knuckles and joints. Once the white dots are in place, draw a wide brush across the hand, and the white oil paint will blend out. This could either be done wet-on-wet or right over the dry paint.

If your head-painting session did not quite turn out as you had anticipated, don't despair – simply strip the paint using a toothbrush and paint remover (PineSol floor cleaner works well), then try the steps again. Have several heads on the go at once, so that you do not fret and waste time waiting for each step to dry. And, if one head gets messed up, you can continue with the other heads without worrying. I can assure you that as time goes on, each new figure will look better than your previous one, and your painting techniques will change and develop. If you don't like the way a head

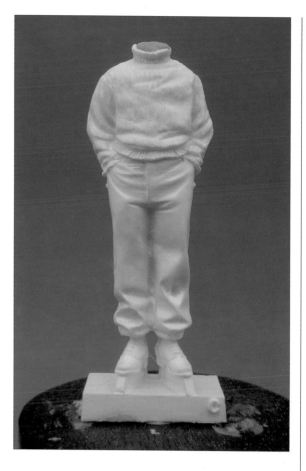

A Yoshi 1/35-scale figure primed and ready for painting in enamels.

After the primer had thoroughly dried, I base painted the sweater in Humbrol No. 144 and the trousers in Humbrol No. 33. I also added a first shadow by adding about 20 per cent Humbrol Matt Black into both base paint colours and blending these into the semi-wet base colours.

A second shadow was applied by adding a bit more Matt Black to the base colours. A first highlight was also applied by adding Humbrol Flesh 61 to the base colours. Dirt and grime (from various Humbrol earth colours) were stippled on the sweater and trousers.

I re-applied some of the original base colour on the sweater on selective areas to tone down the dirt effect. I added a second highlight on the trousers and on the folds of the arms. All that remains is to add a light wash of Payne's Gray to the sweater fringes and collar (see page 56).

turned out, put the figure out of sight for a week. We tend to be most critical of ourselves in the heat of the moment.

Painting tan-water pattern camouflage

Subject:	*Panzertruppen, Russia, 1943*
Modeller:	*Mark Bannerman*
Base kit:	*Tristar Panzer Grenadiers, 1/35 scale, plastic, plus Warriors resin head and boots*
Paints:	*Citadel White primer*
	Humbrol Enamel: Matt Black No.33, Dark Yellow No.94, Matt White No.34, Red Brown No.160, Matt Forest Green No.150, Brown Bess No.170, Dark Earth No.29, Matt Slate Grey No.31
	Winsor & Newton: Titanium White, Raw Umber, Prussian Blue, Mars Black

The first cold-weather combat uniforms were distributed to German Panzer crews during the winter of 1942/43. The two-piece reversible suit appeared in two basic patterns: field grey (sometimes described as mouse grey), and camouflaged. There were several camouflage patterns, including one named *Sumpfmuster*. This has traditionally been referred to in English as 'tan-water' pattern. Werner Palinckx, in his comprehensive book *Camouflage Uniforms of the German Wehrmacht* (Schiffer, 2002), argues 'marsh' pattern is a better translation.

Two variants of the marsh pattern existed: the 43 pattern featured angular, hard-edged splinters of green and brown over the base colour, while the 44 pattern had random green and brown blotches, with fuzzy borders and no hard edges. The base colour for both types was a yellow-tan brown, and the pattern was overlaid with 'rain drop' markings. The jacket and trousers were worn over the uniform field blouse.

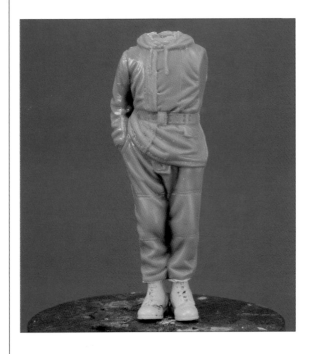

I replaced the boots with the Warriors resin offering.

The neck area was drilled deeper to accommodate a Warriors head.

The figure was primed in Tamiya White primer.

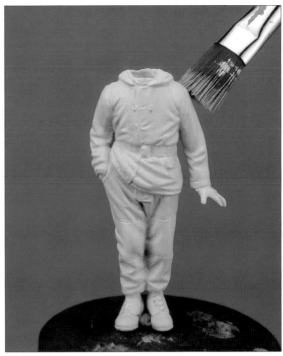

The jacket was painted in a thin layer of Titanium White oil paints and allowed to dry for several days.

A second layer of oil paint was applied by adding a minute amount of Raw Umber and a very tiny speck of Prussian Blue to Titanium White.

I repeated the same step as previously but added about 10 per cent more Raw Umber oil paints to the base colour mix.

Excess paint was removed by vertically brushing downwards on the figure.

Note how shadows are beginning to show as a result of removing excess paint with residual paint being deposited into shadows areas.

The trousers were first base-painted in two thin layers of Humbrol Dark Yellow 94. Some shadows were added using the base colour with a few drops of Matt Black added to the paint.

For the patchy camouflage pattern, I used Humbrol Red Brown No.160 and Dark Green No.86. The paints were heavily diluted in thinners and lightly jabbed onto the trousers.

For this project, I chose a Tristar 1/35-scale plastic figure. I replaced the boots and head with Warriors resin offerings. After the usual clean up and priming, I decided I would paint the figure's jacket in white using oils, and paint the trousers in the reversible marsh 43 pattern using enamels.

I started with the jacket, applying a thick base coat of light grey oil paint using a mix of 85 per cent Titanium White, 15 per cent Raw Umber and a very tiny speck of Prussian Blue. This latter colour is very strong, so the speck should be the size of a typed period. The oil mix was brought to a taupe colour and applied to the entire jacket. I then stroked a wide brush downwards all around the figure, ensuring that the oil paint was spread out and that all highlight points were devoid of any of the taupe colour. The result was the original primer white on the highlight points and a taupe-grey colour in all of the shadow areas.

After the oils had dried (about three days), I sparingly painted all of the highlight points using Titanium White. Once this had dried, I applied a coat of pure Titanium White over the entire jacket, including the previously painted shadows. Once it was applied, I immediately removed the oil paint with a wide brush, leaving a glaze-like film on the jacket. This step accomplishes two things: it lightens the jacket substantially, and blends the highlights and shadows together. Once dry, the last step was to apply some shadows in the very deepest recesses using a shade of Titanium White mixed with Raw Umber in a 3:2 ratio.

The camouflage trousers were first base-painted in two thin layers of Humbrol Enamel Dark Yellow No.94. Before the base paint dried, I added a few shadows to the trousers by stippling with a mixture of the base colour darkened by a few drops of Matt Black No.33. For the patchy camouflage pattern, I used Red Brown No.160 and Matt Forest Green No.150. The paints were heavily diluted in thinners (almost 50:50) and lightly jabbed onto the trousers, using photos from several books as a reference. To shadow the two colours, I added 10 per cent Matt Black to the Red Brown and Forest Green, and carefully stippled the paint into the appropriate shadow areas. I then added 20 per cent Matt White No.34 to the two camouflage base colours, and applied highlights on the very tops of the folds by lightly stippling the brush onto the surface.

Tri-Star's excellent 1/35-scale injection-moulded plastic Panzer Grenadiers figure set.

The trousers were highlighted using a dab of Humbrol Flesh mixed with each of the three colours to pick out the highlights. The last step was adding the 'rain marks' on the camouflage trousers. For this, I used a very fine (sized .01) Dark Green – almost black – architect's felt pen.

Once this was completely dry, I painted the boots and belt in a mixture of Matt Black and Brown Bess No.170 in a 50/50 ratio. The boots were then dry-brushed in Dark Earth No.29. The gloves were painted in an enamel blue-grey mix, washed in Mars Black oils and dry-brushed with Matt Slate Grey No.31. The head was painted in oils and added to the figure.

The last step was the most time-consuming part of the project – adding the 'rain marks' on the camouflage trousers. For this purpose, I used a very fine (sized .01) dark felt pen meant for architects. This can be a bit tricky to apply because the pen may gunk up. The key is to draw the lines very finely and lightly. After applying six or seven lines on the trousers, I would scribble the pen on regular typing paper to keep it from clogging.

For the black Panzer uniform project, I used a combination of two oil paints for the base colour: Ivory Black and Tinted Flesh.

Painting black Panzer uniforms with oils

Subject:	*Panzertruppen, Norway, 1940*
Modeller:	*Mark Bannerman*
Base kit:	*Alpine Miniatures, 1/35 scale, resin, plus Hornet Head, Archer Fine Transfers*
Paints:	*Citadel White primer*
	Lukas Studio: Ivory Black
	Winton: Flesh Tint

In the opening chapter of this book, I used enamels to paint a figure wearing a black Panzer uniform. In this short feature, I will instead use oils on a figure dressed in the same type of uniform. For my subject, I chose an Alpine Miniatures 1/35-scale resin figure with a Hornet head.

Oils are translucent, which allows you to build effects with thin layers of paint. Applying several thin coats, working from light shades to dark, will result in a number of interesting hues and rich tonal values. However, oils generally dry semi-glossy because they contain linseed oil, which is not desirable when painting the matt and muted uniforms of World War II.

There are a few ways to remedy this. One option is to place the oils on a piece of typing paper or an index card. Allow the paper to absorb some of the linseed oil. For a pea-sized blob of oil paint, I usually let it sit on the paper for one hour before using. Another option is to mix in small amounts of Grumbacher Medium I. This medium helps speed up the drying time of oil paints, and reduces glossy finishes. Lastly, an overspray of Tamiya Flat Clear or Testors Dullcote also works well, but should only be applied once the oil paint is perfectly dry.

After clean up and priming, I painted the figure's belt using the leather-painting technique described on page 74. For base-coating a black uniform using oil paints, I mixed 25 per cent Flesh Tint and 75 per cent Ivory Black oil paints. The paint was applied sparingly all over the figure. As soon as the uniform was base-painted and the paint thinned out as much as possible, I removed excess paint by stroking downward with a large, rounded brush.

While the paint was drying, I started in with the shadows by adding 10 per cent more Ivory Black to the base colour. This darker paint was added to all of the shadow areas. I then allowed the figure to sit for about two hours (under an overturned glass to protect it from dust). I started the blending process using

The 1/35-scale resin Alpine Miniatures figure was lightly primed twice in Tamiya White primer.

ABOVE I started with the belt because this would be harder to paint once the uniform was painted. The belt and holster were first 'stained' with a thin application of Winsor & Newton Burnt Sienna. Staining the paint requires jabbing the paint on (instead of stroking the brush) then spreading the paint out as much as possible.

ABOVE RIGHT The rear view after applying a second coat of Sienna.

RIGHT A thin layer of a Black oils mixed with Flesh oils in a ratio of 4:1 was thinly applied to the figure. Note how glossy the oil paints appear when wet.

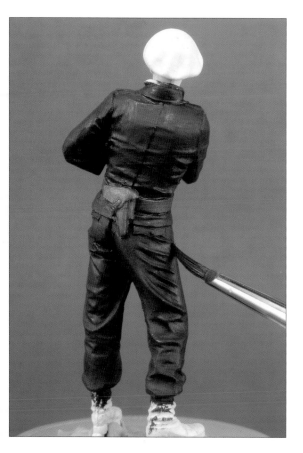

ABOVE LEFT It is important to make certain that the oil paint is applied as thinly as possible. This may require using a second brush to spread out the paint over the surface of the figure.

ABOVE The first highlights were applied using a mix of Ivory Black to Flesh Tint in a ratio of 3:1. The paint should be very thin and applied directly on top of the wet base paint. I also applied a stain of Raw Umber to the belt to darken up the overall appearance of the leather. The head was also painted in oils.

LEFT As soon as the highlights were applied to the tops of the folds, I jabbed a dry round brush to blend the highlights into the base. The jabbing and poking motion is kept very light and controlled.

The result after a second highlight was applied. The second highlight was an equal mix of Ivory Black to Flesh Tint (50:50). The gloves and scarf were painted in Humbrol Matt Tank Grey 67 mixed with 20 per cent Matt White 34. The paint for the boots was the same as that for the uniform.

The collar piping and patch edges were first painted in a thin line of Humbrol Matt White. Once dry, I painted over the white with Winton Alizarin Crimson oil paints. The reason for painting white piping first is that it helps bring out the Crimson colour. Painting a dark colour on a black base will make it difficult to see. The figure was also dull coated to reduce the eggshell finish.

a clean, dry No.2 brush. I lightly stroked the brush on the border between the semi-wet base colour and the freshly applied shadow area. Because all of your work is being done while the oils are wet (termed 'wet-on-wet'), there is no need to use thinners to help blend the two shades. Once the first set of shadows had been added and blended, I added pure Ivory Black into the deepest parts of the recesses. This was further blended out into adjacent paint.

While the whole of the figure was still in a semi-wet state, I added a series of progressively lighter shades of the base colour by adding more Flesh Tint to the base. With each application to the figure's high points, I jabbed the highlight paint into the base to blend out the freshly applied highlight colour. I added four highlight shades, each time adding 10 per cent Flesh Tint, until the last application was approximately a 50:50 combination of Ivory Black and Flesh Tint. While the oil paints are still wet and glossy, the results will not be noticeable. However, once the oil paints dry, over a period of a few days, the various tones will become apparent.

When the oils are perfectly dry, you may notice a slight satin sheen or eggshell finish. This is a normal property of oil paints. A few light oversprays of a flat clear coat such as Tamiya Flat Clear or Testors Dullcote will reduce the sheen. It is critical to ensure the oils are perfectly dry before applying a matt coat, otherwise the matt coat combined with even the slightest wet oil paint will result in a permanently glossy finish on your figure. For this reason, painting in oils requires time and patience. From start to finish, this particular figure was painted over a two-week period in daily sessions of about 10–15 minutes each (totalling about two and a half hours).

For the remainder of the figure, the head was painted in oils using the techniques described elsewhere in this book. The uniform piping was recreated by

OPPOSITE The figure placed on a scenic base with an NbFz in the background.

first painting a thin white border along the lapels with Humbrol Enamel Matt White No.34, then touching up with Winton Alizarin Crimson oil paint. The gloves and scarf were painted in Humbrol Enamel Intermediate Blue No.144, washed in Ivory Black oils and dry-brushed lightly with No.144. The boots were painted in the same way as the uniform, then dry-brushed in various enamel brown shades once the oil paint was perfectly dry.

Painting with oils is not much different from painting with enamels. For some modellers, the biggest drawback with oil paints is that they take several days to dry. However, this can be helpful, because it allows time to make corrections and adjustments. Leaving a figure for a day or two allows you to see small imperfections you overlooked initially.

Weathering clothing

Subject:	Panzer Grenadier, Russia, 1943
Modeller:	Mark Bannerman
Base kit:	Jaguar, 1/35 scale, resin, plus a Hornet head
Paints:	Humbrol Enamel: Matt Flesh No.61, Matt White No.39, Khaki Drill No.72, Dark Earth No.26

Weathering figure clothing is an important step to achieving realism and helps tie the figure to the base and the environment. Many modellers use pastel chalks for weathering, but, unfortunately, they are not the best for depicting prominent wear and tear on uniforms. There are a few reasons for this. Firstly, at close glance, chalks and pastels tend to look as though they are sitting on the surface of the uniform, instead of being ground-in stains and dirt. Secondly, pastels are not permanent, so any exposure or handling could quickly ruin the overall effect. More importantly, pastels can sometimes obliterate well-executed highlights and shadows.

My preferred medium for dirtying clothing is enamels. I find they are the simplest to use, dry extremely flat and are quite manageable. Also, because of the longer drying period of enamels (versus acrylics), the application of enamels can be 'reversed' and corrected, if necessary.

I started to transform the trousers from a 'parade' uniform into weather-beaten, dirty and dusty clothing. Before applying weathering, it is important to consider the terrain, the circumstances, and the degree of weathering you want to achieve. This step can easily be overdone. *(Continues on page 73.)*

A few of the Humbrol Enamel paints for weathering and dirtying up a figure, among them Matt Flesh No.61, Khaki Drill No.72, Dark Earth No.26 and Dark Stone No.187.

I placed a bit of paint on a brush, removed the excess and proceeded to lightly jab the paint onto the trousers.

Different combinations of earth-coloured enamels are jabbed onto the figure's trousers.

ABOVE The result is paint which has been 'ground' into the trousers – similar to real dirt.

RIGHT A simple temporary base for the figure – a DioArt resin wall painted overall in Humbrol Matt Light Grey No.147 then dry-brushed first in Humbrol Matt Brick Red No.70 followed by two successive washes of Raw Umber oils paints. The bricks (by Verlinden) were glued in place with epoxy glue.

The figure was temporarily fixed in place and further but restrained stipples of various earth-coloured paints were applied with a dried-out brush (old dried-out brushes can be very useful for weathering jobs).

A few last touches to ensure it looks uniform and balanced.

The figure was permanently attached to a larger diorama and more dirtying had to be done to balance with the winter muddy Russian road. The lower part of the jacket received further mud and grime using Humbrol Dark Earth.

The upper part of the jacket also received some dirtying with Humbrol Flat Earth and Matt Flesh but the stippling was restrained and kept very light.

To depict dried mud and stained trousers, I used Humbrol Enamel Khaki Drill No.72, Dark Earth No.29 and Matt Flesh No.61. I reached into the bottom of each tin with a toothpick and placed a bit of the residue onto a palette. I started by mixing a bit of Khaki Drill with Dark Earth in a 1:1 ratio. I placed a little paint on a 00 brush, removed the excess (similar to the amount of paint you would typically need on your brush for dry-brushing armour) and proceeded to lightly jab the paint onto the trousers. At first, it may seem as though no paint is adhering at all. This is fine and perfectly normal.

Next, I added a bit of Matt Flesh to the mix, again removed the excess paint, and lightly jabbed the brush onto the same lower area of the trousers, going all the way around the figure. I then added Matt White to the mix and repeated the step. It is best to go from a dark tone on the lower part of the trousers, working your way up, to a lighter tone on the upper section. This depicts dried mud/dirt on the top and fresh mud/dirt at the bottom.

I went back to the trousers to further accentuate the dirty knees as much as possible whilst still keeping it realistic. In this instance, I used two colours: Dark Earth and Matt Flesh. I proceeded with the same technique as above, but kept the paint in one area around the knees. I jabbed Dark Earth straight out of the tin, then added Matt Flesh in minute quantities. The result is that I was able to draw different tones within a very small area.

The trick is to ensure that the paint application is kept very light with each jab, avoiding at all costs scrubbing the brush back and forth, which can polish the paint and leave a glossy finish. The same technique is applied to the elbows and lower part of the jacket, using lighter dirt tones (Khaki Drill mixed with Matt White) to depict dried mud and dirt. Again, always keep as little paint on the brush as possible, and keep it subtle.

If you apply too much dirt, there are two ways to reverse this. You can either 'mute' or cover the effect by jabbing on some of the original uniform base colour to tone it down, or use a little thinner to remove the excess paint while it is still wet. I would suggest the first option, as this carries less risk of messing up your work.

OPPOSITE **The figure is permanently fixed to its new home with a bit of five-minute epoxy. The base work is by Arthur Sekula.**

The precise same weathering technique and Humbrol colours were used to dirty up this 1/35-scale Alhambra figure's bedsheet wrap and trousers.

Painting leather

Painting leather can be an easy task in a few simple steps. On this 1/16-scale Tamiya revolver holster, I applied two light coats of white primer.

I then applied a very thin layer of Burnt Sienna oil paints and removed the excess in a downward flick with the largest brush possible. The result is that the white primer has been stained with a reddish brown colour. Allow to dry for a week.

I mixed equal amounts of Raw Umber and Burnt Sienna oils and brushed this darker shade oil paint on the entire holster. With a large round brush, I removed the excess paint resulting in the darker shade colour finding itself along seams and in shadow areas. This was left to dry for another week.

The item needs to be perfectly dry before applying the third and last application of paint.

I applied Raw Umber oil paint all over the holster and then removed the excess with a large brush. This resulted in a slightly darker shade of leather.

The completed holster attached to a Tamiya figure. By adding more Raw Umber applications or combination mixes of black and/or brown oil paint, many effects can be achieved. This technique can be used on accessories such as boots, belts, rifle stocks and even for painting horses. The trick is to ensure that the primer is white at the outset and that every application of oil paint is left to thoroughly dry before another application is applied.

Kits and accessories

There are hundreds of Panzertruppen figures in all scales available, and it would be virtually impossible to list all of them here. However, here is a list of some excellent manufacturers of resin, metal and plastic Panzertruppen figures available at the time of writing, and sites where these can be viewed and purchased.

Alpine Miniatures   http://www.alpineminiatures.com
Andrea Miniatures   http://www.andrea-miniatures.com
Coree   http://www.redlancers.com
Cromwell Models   http://www.xs4all.nl/~cromwell
DML (Dragon)   http://www.dragon-models.com
GSI Creos   http://www.coloradominiatures.com
Hobby Fan   http://www.redlancers.com
Hornet   http://www.greenwichgateway.com/hornetandwolf

Tamiya's 1/48-scale German infantry figure set.

Tristar's 1/35-scale German self-propelled gun crew.

S&T Products' Afrikakorps Panzer crew figure set (no. 16009) in 1/16 scale, sculpted by John Rosengrant.

Jaguar	http://www.coloradominiatures.com
Mk 35 Figures	http://www.redlancers.com
Modelling Artisan Mori	http://www.coloradominiatures.com
Nemrod	http://www.coloradominiatures.com
New Connections	http://www.redlancers.com
Royal Models	http://www.royalmodel.com
S&T Products	http://www.sntproducts.com
Takahashi	http://www.greenwichgateway.com/hornetandwolf
Tamiya	http://tamiya.com
TANK	http://www.coloradominiatures.com
Tri-Star	http://www.tristarmodel.com
Verlinden	http://www.verlinden-productions.com
Warriors	http://www.vpop.net/~scalmall/warriors.htm
Wolf	http://www.greenwichgateway.com/hornetandwolf

"ACHTUNG-JABO!" PANZER CREW (FRANCE
1:35 '39-'45 SERIES

DRAGON

ABOVE Dragon's Panzer crew set in 1/35 scale.

HANDS 02
3 right, 3 left hands
for 1:35 scale figurines
HORNET

HANDS 03
3 right, 3 left hands
for 1:35 scale figurines
(Trim sprues with care !)
HORNET

HGH 19
5 more heads with
German M1943 field caps
HORNET

HH 11
5 different bareheads
laughing, joking
HORNET

5 heads with WW2
German

HGH10
Heads with WW2 German
mountain troops cap
HORNET

LEFT A selection of the excellent Hornet heads and hands.

Further reading and research

There are many excellent books available to the enthusiast on Panzer crewmen uniforms. The books I found particularly interesting and informative on the subject are listed below.

Bender, Roger and Odegard, Warren *Uniforms, Organizations and History of the Panzertruppe* (ISBN 0-912138-18-1).

Ellis, Chris *The German Army 1933–45* (Ian Allan Publishing, ISBN 0-7110-2193-7).

Gordon-Douglas, S.R. *German Combat Uniforms* (Almark Productions, ISBN 0-85524-016-4).

Hartmann, Theodor *Wehrmacht Divisional Signs* (Almark Publications, ISBN 0-85524-006-7).

Pruett, Michael and Edwards, Robert *Field Uniforms of German Army Panzer Forces in World War 2* (J.J. Fedorowicz Publishing, ISBN 0921199115)

Williamson, Gordon *Panzer Crewman 1939–45*, Warrior Series No. 45 (Osprey Publishing, ISBN 1-84176-328-4).

The only magazine series that I found that covered uniforms almost exclusively was the French-language publication *Armes Militaria*. Although the magazine is a bit of a tough find (unless you live in France or Belgium), most of the articles have been reproduced in hard-bound cover books under the banner of 'Histoire et Collections' and are available on the internet.

There are many excellent websites for re-enactment and uniform reproduction. Some of the more worthy are listed here.

www.Panzerworld.net/uniforms-heerheadgear.html
www.jjfpub.mb.ca/photo_albums.htm
www.thuringenmilitaria.com/uniforms.html
www.lostbattalions.com/german33-45/heer/
    heerlist.html
www.zeltbahn.net/wh_camo.htm
www.militarytour.com/Reproductions/WW11/
    German/RGGermanrepo.htm

Field Uniforms of German Army Panzer Forces in World War 2

Michael H. Pruett & Robert J. Edwards

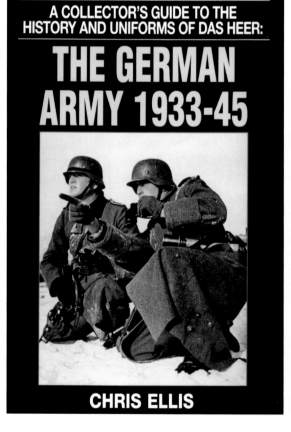

A COLLECTOR'S GUIDE TO THE HISTORY AND UNIFORMS OF DAS HEER:

THE GERMAN ARMY 1933-45

CHRIS ELLIS

Uniforms, Organization and History
of the
PANZERTRUPPE

Roger James Bender
&
Warren W. Odegard

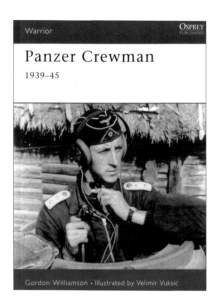

Warrior

OSPREY
PUBLISHING

Panzer Crewman
1939–45

Gordon Williamson · Illustrated by Velimir Vuksic

ARMES
MILITARIA

N°163

MENSUEL - FEVRIER 1999
35 FF/5,34 € - 240 FB - 9,60 FS
6,955 CAN - PORTUGAL CONT. 840 ESC
RCI 3500 FCFA - US $7.95

FRANCE
Avril 45, la journée des drapeaux
Les officiers
des troupes du Levant
1939-1945
Le canon 25 Pdr
Pilote B-17 USAAF
Les Polonais Libres

LUFTWAFFE
Les tenues noires
« Hermann Göring »
La dague d'officier

Index

1.

5.

9.

2.

6.

10.

3.

7.

11.

4.

8.

12.

9. Leather painting

This is the result when Raw Umber is applied over a fully cured application of Burnt Sienna. Note the leather and wood traits of the tone and effect.

5. Flesh base colour

To paint a flesh colour base, I mix three oil colours: Gold Ochre, Burnt Sienna and Titanium White in a 2:1:4 ratio.

1. Black uniform base colour

I used two colours for painting the black Panzer uniforms: Matt Flesh No.61 and Matt Black No.33 in the Humbrol series. I mixed 80 per cent Matt Black No.33 with 20 per cent Matt Flesh No.61 to create the base colour.

10. Bunt Sienna

Pure Winsor & Newton Bunt Sienna can make some very nice hues for flesh and different types of leathers.

6. Flesh highlights

I added 20 per cent Titanium White to the flesh base to create the highlight colour that is applied on the nose bridge, above the eyebrows and on the upper cheeks.

2. Medium highlights (black uniforms)

To make the medium highlights, I mixed a small amount of 30 per cent Matt Flesh to 70 per cent Matt Black on my palette.

11. Summer uniform grey

I use Humbrol Matt Slate Grey No.33 from the tin, which is perfect for German summer tanker uniforms.

7. Titanium White (flesh tones)

Pure Titanium White is a superb medium for making a flesh colour mix lighter in tone.

3. Medium shadows (black uniforms)

The medium shadow shade was created by adding 10 per cent Matt Flesh to 90 per cent Matt Black.

12. White uniforms

I use an oil mix of 85 per cent Titanium White, 15 per cent Raw Umber and a tiny amount of Prussian Blue, for the base of a white uniform.

8. Shadows (flesh tones)

A shadow tone can be created by applying a touch of Burnt Sienna and Gold Ochre to the flesh base.

4. Deep shadows (black uniforms)

The deep shadow areas for the black Panzer uniform was pure Humbrol Matt Black No.33.